Centre

W0246457

INRI

PARALLEL IMAGE ANALYSIS: TOOLS AND MODELS

SERIES IN MACHINE PERCEPTION AND ARTIFICIAL INTELLIGENCE*

Editors: **H. Bunke** (Univ. Bern, Switzerland)
P. S. P. Wang (Northeastern Univ., USA)

*For the complete list of titles in this series, please write to the Publisher.

Series in Machine Perception and Artificial Intelligence – Vol. 31

PARALLEL IMAGE ANALYSIS:
TOOLS AND MODELS

Editors

S Miguet
Université Lumière Lyon 2, France

A Montanvert
Institut Albert Bonniot, France

P S P Wang
Northeastern University, USA

World Scientific
Singapore • New Jersey • London • Hong Kong

Published by

World Scientific Publishing Co. Pte. Ltd.

P O Box 128, Farrer Road, Singapore 912805

USA office: Suite 1B, 1060 Main Street, River Edge, NJ 07661

UK office: 57 Shelton Street, Covent Garden, London WC2H 9HE

British Library Cataloguing-in-Publication Data
A catalogue record for this book is available from the British Library.

PARALLEL IMAGE ANALYSIS: TOOLS AND MODELS

ISBN 981-02-3458-9

Printed in Singapore by Uto-Print

CONTENTS

PREFACE

SERGE MIGUET

Laboratory E.R.I.C., bâtiment L, Université Lumière Lyon 2
5, avenue Pierre Mendes, 69676 Bron Cedex, France

ANNICK MONTANVERT

Institut Albert Bonniot
TIMC – INFODIS, Domáine de la Merci
F-38700 LaFronche, France

P. S. P. WANG

College of Computer Science, Northeastern University
Boston, MA 02115, USA

The contributions of this book were presented at the International Workshop on Parallel Image Analysis, organized on December 7th and 8th, 1995 at the Laboratoire de l'Informatique du Parallélisme of the Ecole Normale Supérieure de Lyon, France. This conference was the fourth edition of a successful series of workshops dedicated to models, algorithms, and architectures for parallel image processing. Previous editions have taken place in Paris, France in 1991, Ube, Japan in 1992 and Washington DC, USA in 1994.

From the 23 papers that were presented at the workshop, 8 were selected by prominent professionals and experts mainly from the USA, Japan, United Kingdom, Switzerland and France. This book is representative of the traditional topics of the workshop, from theoretical models for parallel image analysis to real life applications implemented on parallel multi-computers. The papers can roughly be divided into four parts:

1. **Theoretical models for parallel image recognition.** The first paper "Nonclosure Properties of Two-dimensional One-Marker Automata" by Ito, Inoue and Wang establishes new results on Blum and Hewitt's 2D automata dedicated to picture recognition. The next paper "Parallel Distributed Detection of Invariant Feature Associated with Self-Similar Patterns" by Kamejima, presents a distributed scheme for identifying self-similar pictures, and shows an application to dynamic recognition of fractal patterns.

2. **Tools for parallel image processing.** The first paper of this part "Parallel Tools for Colored Images Processing", by Lozano, Ubéda and Vigouroux, presents a general framework for processing large color images like textile pictures on conventional workstation clusters under the PVM environment. The second paper by Robin, Privat and Renaudin entitled "Asynchronous Relaxation of Morphological Operators: a Joint Architecture-Algorithm Perspective" presents an idea issued from an active area of research in VLSI design, the asynchronous circuits. These concepts allow to improve the convergence of the widely used morphological operators.

1

3. **Parallel algorithms for computer graphics.** The third part of this book is dedicated to image synthesis. The first paper by Renaud "Fast Local and Global Illuminations through a SIMD Z-Buffer", presents a parallel implementation of the well known depth buffer algorithm on a Maspar MP-1 machine, and its use for a global illumination projective radiosity algorithm. The second paper of this part is entitled "A Load Balanced Parallel Ground Visualization Tool". Contassot-Vivier presents a data allocation strategy and a dynamic load-balancing scheme for the problem of visualizing texture-mapped Digital Elevation Models on a MIMD distributed memory machine.

4. **3D medical imaging in parallel.** This last section of the publication contains two papers related to the domain of 3D medical imaging. Reissman and Magnin propose in their paper entitled "Modeling 3D Deformable Objects with the Active Pyramid", a multiresolution method associated to a matching strategy for modeling elastic 2D or 3D objects at different scales. Finally, the paper "Complexity Analysis of a Parallel Implementation of the Marching-Cubes algorithm" by Miguet and Nicod presents a bound on the complexity of the surface extracted by this well known 3D segmentation algorithm. This analysis is exploited for optimizing the use of different processors in the parallel version of the algorithm.

We wish to thank all the authors for their contributions and the members of the program committee, without which this book also published as a special issue of the International Journal of Pattern Recognition would not have been possible. We thank also all our sponsors for their help: the *Centre National pour la Recherche Scientifique* (CNRS), the *Ministère de l'Enseignement Supérieur et de la Recherche* (MESR), and the Joined Research Programs *Parallélisme, Réseaux et Systèmes* (PRS) and *Traitement du Signal et de l'Image* (TDSI) of the CNRS and the MESR.

NONCLOSURE PROPERTIES OF
TWO-DIMENSIONAL ONE-MARKER AUTOMATA

AKIRA ITO, KATSUSHI INOUE and YUE WANG

Department of Computer Science and Systems Engineering
Faculty of Engineering, Yamaguchi University, Ube 755, Japan
E-mail: ito@csse.yamaguchi-u.ac.jp

Several nonclosure properties of each class of sets accepted by two-dimensional alternating one-marker automata, alternating one-marker automata with only universal states, nondeterministic one-marker automata, deterministic one-marker automata, alternating finite automata, and alternating finite automata with only universal states are shown. To do this, we first establish the upper bounds of the working space used by "three-way" alternating Turing machines with only universal states to simulate those "four-way" non-storage machines. These bounds provide us a simplified and unified proof method for the whole variants of one-marker and/or alternating finite state machine, without directly analyzing the complex behavior of the individual four-way machine on two-dimensional rectangular input tapes. We also summarize the known closure properties including Boolean closures for all the variants of two-dimensional alternating one-marker automata.

Keywords: Automaton, two-dimensional tape, connected picture, one-marker, closure property, alternation, Turing machine.

1. INTRODUCTION

After the work of Blum and Hewitt,[1] the study of two-dimensional automata, i.e. automata equipped with two-dimensional rectangular input tapes rather than ordinary one-dimensional strings, has been done by several researchers[18,19] (for various applications of two-dimensional automata and language theory to picture recognition, see Refs. 20 and 21). Among their outcomes, the properties of deterministic finite automata (DFs) and nondeterministic finite automata (NFs) are considerably revealed: For instance, it is known[4,6,9] that the classes of sets accepted by DFs and NFs are both not closed under each such operation as row (column) catenation, row (column) closure, row (column) cyclic closure, or projection.

On the other hand, little is known about the properties of two-dimensional one-marker (otherwise called one-pebble) automata,[1] which is generally considered[18] to be a weakest sequential recognizer of the connectedness of two-dimensional binary pictures.[1] Especially, none of the closure properties of these deterministic and nondeterministic one-markers had ever been known until now, except about trivial Boolean operations.

Parallel Image Analysis: Tools and Models (1998) 3–28
© World Scientific Publishing Company

The main purpose of this paper is to show several nonclosure properties of two-dimensional one-marker automata, extending the nondeterministic concept to alternating one, which was first proposed in Ref. 10 for two-dimensional automata study.

To this end, Sec. 3 first investigates the sufficient spaces for "three-way alternating Turing machines with only universal states" (3UTs)[13] to simulate one-marker (and alternating) automata. For example, we will show that $2^{O(n)}$ $(O(n^2))$ space is sufficient for 3UTs to simulate alternating one-marker automata (alternating one-marker automata with only universal states).

From these results, Sec. 4 proves the nonclosure properties of the class of sets accepted by each variant of two-dimensional alternating one-marker automata under row (column) catenation, row (column) closure, row (column) cyclic closure, and projection operation. Section 4 also gives the closure properties under Boolean operations.

The final section summarizes the closure properties of two-dimensional alternating one-marker automata, including finite state machines.

2. DEFINITIONS

Prior to our main subject, this section gives the rigorous definitions and notations of two-dimensional marker automata.

2.1. Two-Dimensional Tapes and Operations on Them

Definition 2.1. Let Σ be a finite set of symbols. A *two-dimensional tape* over Σ is a two-dimensional rectangular array of elements of Σ. The set of all two-dimensional tapes over Σ is denoted by Σ^{2+}. Given a tape $x \in \Sigma^{2+}$, $l_1(x)$ denotes the number of rows of x and $l_2(x)$ denotes the number of columns of x. If $1 \leq i \leq l_1(x)$ and $1 \leq j \leq l_2(x)$, we let $x(i,j)$ denote the symbol in x with coordinates (i,j). Furthermore, we define

$$x[(i,j),(i',j')],$$

when $1 \leq i \leq i' \leq l_1(x)$ and $1 \leq j \leq j' \leq l_2(x)$, as the two-dimensional tape z satisfying the following:

(i) $l_1(z) = i' - i + 1$ and $l_2(z) = j' - j + 1$,
(ii) for each k, r $[1 \leq k \leq l_1(z)$ and $1 \leq r \leq l_2(z)]$,

$$z(k,r) = x(k+i-1, r+j-1).$$

For any $x \in \Sigma^{2+}$, the ith row $x[(i,1),(i,l_1(x))]$ of x is simply denoted by $x[i,*]$.

The operations on two-dimensional tapes we consider here are an analogy of standard operations on one-dimensional strings such as concatenation, Kleene closure, length-preserving homomorphism, or reversal operation.[3] These two-dimensional operations were introduced in Ref. 17 originally for the study of array grammars.

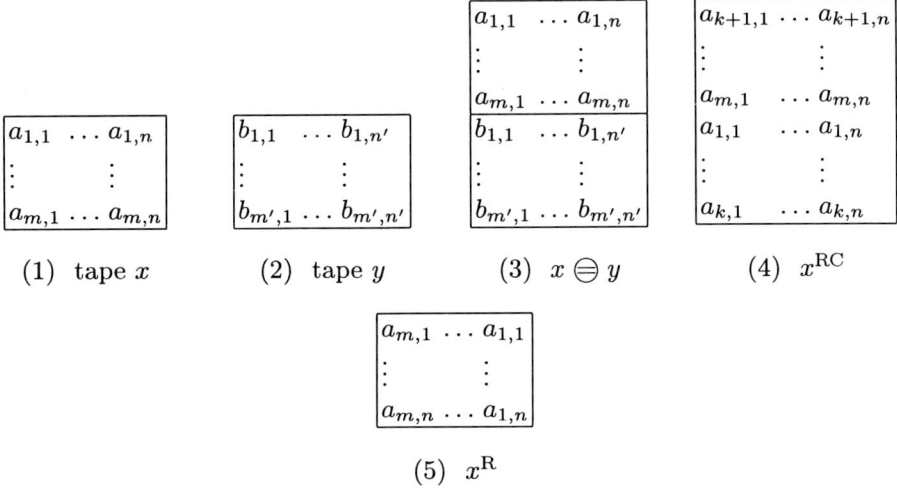

Fig. 1. Operations on two-dimensional tapes.

Definition 2.2.[2] Let x, y be two-dimensional tapes with $l_1(x) = m$ and $l_2(x) = n$ and $l_1(y) = m'$ and $l_2(y) = n'$. The *row catenation* $x \ominus y$ of x and y is defined when $n = n'$ and given by the two-dimensional tape z with $l_1(z) = m + m'$ and $l_2(z) = n$ satisfying (1) $z(i, j) = x(i, j)$ for each $i, j (1 \le i \le m, 1 \le j \le n)$ and (2) $z(i + m, j) = y(i, j)$ for each $i, j (1 \le i \le m', 1 \le j \le n)$. A *row cyclic closure* x^{RC} of x is a two-dimensional tape z with the same size as x and satisfying $z(i, j) = x((i + k - 1) \bmod m + 1, j)$ for each $i, j (1 \le i \le m, 1 \le j \le n)$ for some integer $k (1 \le k \le m)$. The *rotation* x^R of x is the two-dimensional tape z with the same size as x and satisfying $z(i, j) = x(j, m - i + 1)$ for each $i, j (1 \le i \le m, 1 \le j \le n)$. Figure 1 above depicts these operations.

The column catenation of x and y and a column cyclic closure of x are similarly defined.

Definition 2.3.[2] Let T, T' be the sets of two-dimensional tapes. Define

$$T \ominus T' = \{\text{the row catenation } x \ominus y \text{ of } x \text{ and } y \mid x \in T \text{ and } y \in T'\}.$$
$$(\textit{row catenation of } T \textit{ and } T'),$$
$$T^{RC} = \{\text{a row cyclic closure } x^{RC} \text{ of } x \mid x \in T\} \quad (\textit{row cyclic closure of } T),$$
$$T^+ = \cup_{0 < i < \infty} T^i \qquad\qquad\qquad (\textit{row closure of } T),$$

where $T^1 = T$ and $T^i = T^{i-1} \ominus T$ $(i \ge 2)$.

The *column catenation* of T and T', the *row cyclic closure* of T, and the *column closure* of T are similarly defined.

Definition 2.4.[7] Let Σ, Δ be the sets of symbols. For any symbol-to-symbol mapping $\tau : \Sigma \mapsto \Delta$, the projection $\bar{\tau} : \Sigma^{2+} \mapsto \Delta^{2+}$ is an extension of τ to the tape-to-tape mapping as follows: For each $x \in \Sigma^{2+}$,

(1) $l_1(\overline{\tau}(x)) = l_1(x)$ and $l_2(\overline{\tau}(x)) = l_2(x)$, and

(2) for each $i, j (1 \le i \le l_1(x), 1 \le j \le l_2(x)), \overline{\tau}(x)(i,j) = \tau(x(i,j))$.

The projection $\overline{\tau}$ is further extended to the mapping on sets of two-dimensional tapes: For a set T of two-dimensional tapes over Σ, define $\overline{\tau}(T) = \{\overline{\tau}(x) \mid x \in T\}$.

Furthermore, we recall the standard notation of complementation operation. For any class $\mathcal{L}$ of the sets of two-dimensional tapes, define

$$\text{co-}\mathcal{L} = \{\text{the complement of } T \mid T \in \mathcal{L}\}.$$

2.2. Two-Dimensional Alternating Marker Automata

In this paper, we mainly deal with one-maker and zero-marker automata, but we introduce more general multi-marker automaton here.[14] Intuitively, a two-dimensional multi-marker automata is a two-dimensional finite automaton which can make marks on its input with restriction that a bounded number of these marks can exist at any time.

Definition 2.5. Let k be a non-negative integer. A *two-dimensional alternating k-marker automaton* (AMk) is a septuple

$$M = (Q, q_0, U, F, \Sigma, \{0,1\}, \delta)$$

where

(1) Q is a finite set of *states*,

(2) $q_0 \in Q$ is the *initial state*,

(3) $U \subseteq Q$ is a set of *universal states*,

(4) $F \in Q$ is a set of *accepting states*,

(5) Σ is a finite *input alphabet*,

(6) $\{0,1\}$ is the *presence and absence* signs of markers,

(7) $\delta \subseteq ((Q \times \{0,1\}^k) \times ((\Sigma \cup \{\#\}) \times \{0,1\}^k)) \times ((Q \times \{0,1\}^k) \times ((\Sigma \cup \{\#\}) \times \{0,1\}^k) \times \Delta)$ is the *next move relation* satisfying the following (where $\# \notin \Sigma$ is the *boundary symbol* and $\Delta = \{\text{up, down, left, right, stationary}\}$ is the direction set of input head):

For any $q, q' \in Q, a, a' \in \Sigma, \mathbf{u} = (u_1, \ldots, u_k), \mathbf{u}' = (u'_1, \ldots, u'_k), \mathbf{v} = (v_1, \ldots, v_k), \mathbf{v}' = (v'_1, \ldots, v'_k) \in \{0,1\}^k$, and $d \in \Delta$, if $([q', \mathbf{u}'], [a', \mathbf{v}'], d) \in \delta([q, \mathbf{u}], [a, \mathbf{v}])$, then (i) $a = a'$ and (ii) for each $i(1 \le i \le k)$,

$$(u_i, v_i, u'_i, v'_i) \in \{(1,0,1,0), (1,0,0,1), (0,0,0,0), (0,1,0,1), (0,1,1,0)\}.$$

A state q in $Q-U$ is said to be *existential*. The machine M has a read-only rectangular input tape with boundary symbols "#"s. If the input head falls off boundaries of the input tape, then the machine M can make no further move.

An element of $Q \times \{0,1\}^k$ is called an *extended state*.

An element of $\Sigma \times \{0,1\}^k$ is called an *extended input symbol* (the set $\Sigma \times \{0,1\}^k$ itself is called *extended input alphabet*). An extended state $[q, \mathbf{u}]$ represents the situation that M is in state q and M holds or does not hold the ith marker in the finite control, according to the value of u_i which is equal to 1 when M holds the marker. An extended input symbol $[a, \mathbf{v}]$ represents the situation that the input symbol on the current cell is a and the ith marker exists on the same cell, according to the value of v_i which is equal to 1 when the marker exists.

Therefore, the condition (ii) of δ implies the following: ① When holding the marker, M can either continue to hold it or put it down on the current cell. ② When not holding the marker, and (a) if there does not exist the marker on the current cell, M cannot create a new marker, but (b) if there exists the marker on the current cell, M can either leave it alone or pick it up.

Definition 2.6. Let $M = (Q, q_0, U, F, \Sigma, \{0, 1\}, \delta)$ be an AMk. An *extended input tape* $\tilde{x}$ of M is a two-dimensional tape obtained from the original input tape x such that

(1) $\tilde{x} \in (\Sigma \times \{0, 1\}^k)^{2+}$,
(2) $l_1(\tilde{x}) = l_1(x)$ and $l_2(\tilde{x}) = l_2(x)$, and
(3) for each $i, j (1 \leq i \leq l_1(\tilde{x}), 1 \leq j \leq l_2(\tilde{x}))$, $\tilde{x}(i, j) = (x(i, j), \mathbf{v})$, where $\mathbf{v} \in \{0, 1\}^k$.

That is, $\tilde{x}$ is a two-dimensional tape over the extended input alphabet each cell of which is a pair of the same symbol as in the given input tape and a 0-1 vector of length k which indicates the presence or absence of the individual k markers.

The *initial input tape* x^0 of M is an extended input tape $\tilde{x}$ such that for each $i, j (1 \leq i \leq l_1(\tilde{x}), 1 \leq j \leq l_2(\tilde{x}))$, $\tilde{x}(i, j) = (x(i, j), \mathbf{0})$, where $\mathbf{0} = (0, 0, \ldots, 0)$, i.e. there is no marker on the input tape.

Definition 2.7. Let $M = (Q, q_0, U, F, \Sigma, \{0, 1\}, \delta)$ be an AMk. A *configuration* of M on x is an element of

$$(\Sigma \times \{0, 1\}^k)^{2+} \times (Q \times \{0, 1\}^k) \times \mathbf{N}^2,$$

where $\mathbf{N}$ is the set of all natural numbers. The first component $\tilde{x}$ of configuration $c = (\tilde{x}, [q, \mathbf{u}], (i, j))$ is an extended input tape of M. The second component $[q, \mathbf{u}]$ of c is an extended state of M. The third component (i, j) of c is the input head position of M. If q is the state associated with configuration c, then c is said to be *universal (existential, accepting) configuration* if q is a universal (existential, accepting) state. The *initial configuration* of M on x is

$$I_M(x) = (x^0, [q_0, \mathbf{1}], (1, 1)),$$

where $\mathbf{1} = (1, 1, \ldots, 1)$, i.e. all markers remain in the finite control of M.

Definition 2.8. Given $M = (Q, q_0, U, F, \Sigma, \{0, 1\}, \delta)$, we write

$$c \vdash_M c'$$

and say c' is a successor of c if configuration c' follows from configuration c in one step of M, according to the transition rules δ. $\vdash_M^*$ denotes the reflexive transitive closure of $\vdash_M$. A *computation path* of M on x is a sequence

$$c_0 \vdash_M c_1 \vdash_M \cdots \vdash_M c_n \ (n \geq 1).$$

A *computation tree* of M is a nonempty labeled tree with the properties,

(1) each node π of the tree is labeled with a configuration $\ell(\pi)$,
(2) if π is an internal node (a nonleaf) of the tree, $\ell(\pi)$ is universal and

$$\{c \mid \ell(\pi) \vdash_M c\} = \{c_1, \ldots, c_k\},$$

then π has exactly k children $\rho_1, \ldots, \rho_k$ such that $\ell(\rho_i) = c_i$,
(3) if π is an internal node of the tree and $\ell(\pi)$ is existential, then π has exactly one child ρ such that

$$\ell(\pi) \vdash_M \ell(\rho).$$

An *accepting computation tree* of M on x is a finite computation tree whose root is labeled with $I_M(x)$ and whose leaves are all labeled with accepting configurations. We say that M *accepts* x if there is an accepting computation tree of M on input x. Define

$$T(M) = \{x \in \Sigma^{2+} \mid M \text{ accepts } x\}.$$

Nondeterministic automaton is a special case of alternating automaton, i.e. it has no universal states (its computation is represented by a computation path). Conversely, alternating automaton which has no existential states is called *alternating automaton with only universal states*. Of course, *deterministic automaton* is a special case of alternating automaton, i.e. each of whose configurations has at most one successor.

By "DMk" ("NMk", "UMk") we denote a deterministic two-dimensional k-marker automaton (a nondeterministic two-dimensional k-marker automaton, an alternating two-dimensional k-marker automaton with only universal states).

The class of sets accepted by AMks is defined as follows.

$$\mathcal{L}[\text{AM}k] = \{T \mid T = T(M) \text{ for some AM}k M\}.$$

$\mathcal{L}[\text{DM}k], \mathcal{L}[\text{NM}k]$, and $\mathcal{L}[\text{UM}k]$ are defined similarly.

Note that an alternating two-dimensional finite automaton[10] is a special case of multi-marker automaton, i.e., equivalent to AM0. By "AF" ("DF","NF","UF") we denote an alternating two-dimensional finite automata (a deterministic two-dimensional finite automaton, a nondeterministic two-dimensional finite automaton, an alternating two-dimensional finite automaton with only universal states). $\mathcal{L}[\text{AF}], \mathcal{L}[\text{DF}], \mathcal{L}[\text{NF}]$, and $\mathcal{L}[\text{UF}]$ denote the classes of sets accepted by the corresponding machines.

The separation result between zero-marker and one-marker of each class is easily derived:

Theorem 2.1.

(1) $\mathcal{L}[\text{DF}] \subsetneq \mathcal{L}[\text{DM1}]$,

(2) $\mathcal{L}[\text{NF}] \subsetneq \mathcal{L}[\text{NM1}]$,

(3) $\mathcal{L}[\text{UF}] \subsetneq \mathcal{L}[\text{UM1}]$,

(4) $\mathcal{L}[\text{AF}] \subsetneq \mathcal{L}[\text{AM1}]$.

Proof. It is shown in Ref. 15 that there exists a set T of square tapes such that $T \notin \mathcal{L}[\text{AF}]$. On the other hand, $T \in \mathcal{L}[\text{DM1}]$ is almost trivial, which implies the theorem. $\qquad\square$

2.3. Alternating Three-way Turing Machines

A three-way Turing machine[7] is viewed as a natural extension of one-dimensional one-way (off line) Turing machine to two-dimension, except that rectangular input tapes are given and that its input head can move left, right, down, but not up on the given input tape. Of course, it has a one-dimensional working tape and a read-write working tape head on it. Two-dimensional three-way Turing machines we treat here are *three-way nondeterministic Turing machines* (3NTs)[7] and *three-way alternating Turing machines with only universal states* (3UTs).[13] For any three-way Turing machine $3X\text{T}$ ($X \in \{\text{N}, \text{U}\}$) M, we say that M is $f(n)$ *space-bounded* if, when M accepts the input x, there exists an accepting computation tree at each node of which no more than $f(n)$ cells of the working tape are used, where n is the number of columns of the rectangular tape x. Let "$3X\text{T}(f(n))$" denote a $f(n)$ space-bounded $3X\text{T}$ and let $\mathcal{L}[3X\text{T}(L(n))]$ denote the class of sets accepted by $3X\text{T}(L(n))$s ($X \in \{\text{N}, \text{U}\}$). We recall the basic relationship between 3UTs and 3NTs under the same space bounds.

Definition 2.9.[12] For a function $f : \mathbf{N} \mapsto \mathbf{N}$, we say that f is a *fully space constructible*, if there exists a one-dimensional off-line Turing machine M such that, for each n, M uses exactly $f(n)$ cells of the storage tape and halts for any input string of length n.

Proposition 2.1.[14] For any fully space constructible function $L(n) \geq \log n$, $3\text{NT}(L(n))$ and $3\text{UT}(L(n))$ can be converted to those machines which always halt, i.e. any computation of which has no loop for any input.

Lemma 2.1.[14] For any fully space constructible function $L(n) \geq \log n$,

$$\mathcal{L}[3\text{UT}(L(n))] = \text{co--}\mathcal{L}[3\text{NT}(L(n))].$$

3. PRELIMINARY RESULTS

The goal of this section is to obtain the upper bounds of the space of three-way alternating Turing machines with only universal states (3UTs) to simulate one-marker automata. We first derive the corresponding space bounds of three-way "nondeterministic" Turing machines (3NTs).

Definition 3.1. Let M be a AM1 and x be an input tape for M. For any $i, j (1 \le i \le l_1(x), 1 \le j \le l_2(x))$, let $x^{+\langle i,j \rangle}$ denote the extended input tape $\tilde{x}$ of x such that (1) $\tilde{x}(i,j) = (x(i,j), 1)$ and (2) for each $(i', j')(\ne (i,j))$, $\tilde{x}(i', j') = (x(i,j), 0)$. That is, $x^{+\langle i,j \rangle}$ is the extended input tape representing the situation in which the marker of M locates on the coordinates (i, j) of the input tape x.

Theorem 3.1.

$$(1) \; \mathcal{L}[\text{DM1}] \subseteq \mathcal{L}[\text{3NT}(n \log n)],$$

$$(2) \; \mathcal{L}[\text{NM1}] \subseteq \mathcal{L}[\text{3NT}(n^2)],$$

$$(3) \; \mathcal{L}[\text{UM1}] \subseteq \mathcal{L}[\text{3NT}(n^2)],$$

$$(4) \; \mathcal{L}[\text{AM1}] \subseteq \cup_{c>0}\mathcal{L}[\text{3NT}(2^{cn})].$$

Proof. The part (1) and part (2) are proved in Theorems 3.1 and 3.2 of Ref. 17, respectively.

    Proof of the part (3): The outline of the simulation is similar to that of the part (2), except that the requirement of the check whether or not the given UM1 ever enters a loop. Suppose a UM1 M and input tape x with $l_1(x) = m$ and $l_2(x) = n$ are given. Without loss of generality, we assume that it starts to move at the rightmost boundary symbol of the bottom boundary row of x, i.e. at the position $(m+1, n+1)$, and that when M accepts an input x, it enters an accepting state at the same position $(m + 1, n + 1)$ with the marker held in the finite control.

    Let Q be the set of states of the finite control of M. For each $i(0 \le i \le m+1)$, define the mappings

$$g_i^{\uparrow-}, g_i^{\downarrow-}, g_i^{\uparrow+} : Q \times \{0, 1, \ldots, n+1\} \mapsto \mathcal{P}(Q \times \{0, 1, \ldots, n+1\})$$

as follows.[a]

$g_i^{\uparrow-}(q, j) = \{(q_1, j_1), (q_2, j_2), \ldots, (q_d, j_d)\}$

    $\Leftrightarrow$ There exist a finite computation tree t of M on x such that (1) the root of t is labeled with the configuration $(x^0, [q, 0], (i - 1, j))$, which means that the marker exists neither on the input tape nor in the finite control of M, (2) all internal nodes of t are labeled with configurations $(x^0, [q', 0], (i', j'))$, where $q' \in Q, j' \in \{0, 1, \ldots, n+1\}$ and $0 \le i' \le i-1$, and (3) each leaf of t is labeled with one of the configurations $(x^0, [q_1, 0], (i, j_1)), (x^0, [q_2, 0], (i, j_2)), \ldots,$ and $(x^0, [q_d, 0], (i, j_d))$.

---

[a] For any set A, $\mathcal{P}(A)$ denotes the power set of A.

$g_i^{\downarrow-}(q,j) = \{(q_1,j_1),(q_2,j_2),\ldots,(q_d,j_d)\}$
   $\Leftrightarrow$ There exist a finite computation tree t of M on x such that (1) the root
   of t is labeled with the configuration $(x^0,[q,0],(i+1,j))$, (2) all internal
   nodes of t are labeled with configurations $(x^0,[q',0],(i',j'))$, where $q' \in Q$,
   $j' \in \{0,1,\ldots,n+1\}$ and $i+1 \le i' \le m+1$, and (3) each leaf of t is labeled
   with one of the configurations $(x^0,[q_1,0],(i,j_1)),(x^0,[q_2,0],(i,j_2)),\ldots,$ and
   $(x^0,[q_d,0],(i,j_d))$.

$g_i^{\uparrow+}(q,j) = \{(q_1,j_1),(q_2,j_2),\ldots,(q_d,j_d)\}$
   $\Leftrightarrow$ There exist a finite computation tree t of M on x such that (1) the root
   of t is labeled with the configuration $(x^0,[q,1],(i-1,j))$, (2) all internal
   nodes of t are labeled with configurations $(x',[q',u'],(i',j'))$ where $q' \in Q$,
   $j' \in \{0,1,\ldots,n+1\}$ and either (i) $x' = x^0$, $u' = 1$, $0 \le i' \le i-1$ or
   (ii) $x' = x^{+\langle i'',j''\rangle}$, $u' = 0$, $i' \in \{0,1,\ldots,m+1\}$ for some $i'',j''(0 \le i'' \le
   i-1, 0 \le j'' \le n+1)$, and (3) each leaf of t is labeled with one of the con-
   figurations $(x^0,[q_1,1],(i,j_1)),(x^0,[q_2,1],(i,j_2)),\ldots,$ and $(x^0,[q_d,1],(i,j_d))$.

It is clear that $O(n)\cdot\log 2^{O(n)} = O(n^2)$ space suffices in order to record these tables
$g_i^{\uparrow+}$, $g_i^{\uparrow-}$, and $g_i^{\downarrow-}$ for each i.

Roughly speaking, a 3NTM' accepting $T(M)$ acts as follows: While scanning
from the top row down to the bottom row of the input, on the ith row M' guesses
$g_i^{\downarrow-}$, constructs both $g_{i+1}^{\uparrow-}$ and $g_{i+1}^{\uparrow+}$, checks $g_{i-1}^{\downarrow-}$, and finally at the $m+1$st row, M'
decides whether or not M accepts x by using the two tables $g_{m+1}^{\uparrow-}$ and $g_{m+1}^{\uparrow+}$.

First, set $g_0^{\uparrow-} = \emptyset$ and $g_0^{\uparrow+} = \emptyset$.
For $i = 0$ to $m+1$ repeat the following:

0) Go to the ith row.
1) Guess $g_i^{\downarrow-}$ arbitrarily, except that when $i = m+1$ set $g_{m+1}^{\downarrow-} = \emptyset$.
2) [compute $g_{i+1}^{\uparrow+}$ from $g_i^{\uparrow-}$, $g_i^{\uparrow+}$, and $g_i^{\downarrow-}$ (for $i \ne m+1$)]

   For each $(q,j) \in Q\times\{0,1,\ldots,n+1\}$, do the following to compute $g_{i+1}^{\uparrow+}(q,j)$:
initialize $g_{i+1}^{\uparrow+}(q,j) = \emptyset$ and begin to perform depth-first search (or any other
tree search method) of the computation tree t of M whose root is labeled with
the configuration $(x^0,[q,1],(i,j))$. During the search, if it is found that M enters
a loop, then set $g_{i+1}^{\uparrow+}(q,j)$ to empty and start a new search of the tree associated with the next state-column-position pair. (The detection of a loop can be
done by the check whether the number of steps of M on the ith row exceeds
$(n+2)\cdot|Q|$.)

   If M goes up to the $i-1$st row at the j'th column with the marker held in the
finite control and enters state q', then refer to the table $g_i^{\uparrow+}(q',j')$ to know the behavior of M above the ith row: if $g_i^{\uparrow+}(q',j')$ is empty, then set $g_{i+1}^{\uparrow+}(q,j)$ to empty
too and start a new search of the tree associated with the next state-column-
position pair. Otherwise, thus $g_i^{\uparrow+}(q',j') = \{(q_1,j_1),(q_2,j_2),\ldots,(q_k,j_k)\} \ne \emptyset$,
then act as if the node labeled with $(x^0,[q',1],(i-1,j'))$ has k direct sons la-
beled with $(x^0,[q_1,1],(i,j_1)),(x^0,[q_2,1],(i,j_2)),\ldots,$ and $(x^0,[q_k,1],(i,j_k))$ and
continue the tree search.

When M goes down to the $i + 1$st row at the j'th column with the marker held in the finite control and is in the state q' after that, add the pair (q', j') to the leaf-node list $g_{i+1}^{\uparrow+}(q, j)$, and backtrack to its predecessor.

If M puts the marker down on the ith row at the kth column and enters state p, then begin to search the inner tree t' whose root is labeled with the configuration $(x^{+\langle i,k \rangle}, [p, 0], (i, k))$ and each of whose leaves is labeled with a configuration $d = (x^0, [p', 1], (i', k'))$ such that $(x^{+\langle i,k \rangle}, [p'', 0], (i, k)) \vdash_M d$ for some $p', p'' \in Q$ and $i', k'(i - 1 \leq i \leq i + 1, k - 1 \leq k' \leq k + 1)$, i.e. d is the configuration in which M will pick up the marker again. Those leaves of t' found in the search are recorded in a list $leaf(t')$. During the simulation, if M goes up to the $i-1$st row or goes down to the $i + 1$st row, then refer to the respective table $g_i^{\uparrow-}$ or $g_i^{\downarrow-}$. Of course, when the corresponding block of the table is empty, set $g_{i+1}^{\uparrow+}(q, j)$ to empty too and start a new search of the tree associated with the next state-column-position pair. When the inner tree search completes and it returns to the root of the tree t', regard all the elements of the resulting list $leaf(t')$ as the direct sons of the configuration $(x^{+\langle i,k \rangle}, [p, 0], (i, k))$ and continue the original tree search of t.

When the search completes and thus it returns to the root of tree t, then proceed to a new tree search associated with the next state-column-position pair.

3) Compute $g_{i+1}^{\uparrow-}$ from $g_i^{\uparrow-}$ (for $i \neq m + 1$), by the method similar to that of $g_{i+1}^{\uparrow+}$ as shown in (2) above. The details are omitted here.

4) Check the validity of $g_{i-1}^{\downarrow-}$ guessed at the previous row (for $i \neq 0$) by temporally creating a new table $\widehat{g_{-i}^{\downarrow-}}$ from $g_{i-1}^{\downarrow-}$ and checking its equality to $g_i^{\downarrow-}$ guessed at the current row. Details are omitted here.

After the program above is executed, M' determines on the $m+1$st row whether the computation tree of M is an accepting tree. To do so, utilizing the two tables $g_{m+1}^{\uparrow-}$ and $g_{m+1}^{\uparrow+}$, M' performs a depth-first search of the tree whose root is labeled with the initial configuration $(x^0, [q_0, 1], (m + 1, n + 1))$ and verifies that all the leaves are labeled with some accepting configuration $(x^0, [q_f, 1], (m + 1, n + 1))$, where q_f is an accepting state of M, and that the tree is not infinite. If these checks succeed, then M' accepts x. Otherwise, M' rejects x.

It will be obvious that $T(M) = T(M')$. Now, consider the amount of space used in the depth-first searches. The stack height for each search is at most $O(n)$, whereas each element of the stack is of size $O(n)$. Thus, the total space used by M' is never beyond $O(n^2)$.

Proof of the part (4): The simulation method is the combination of the part (2) and part (3), since in this case the simulated machines have both universal and existential states. Suppose a AM1 $M = (Q, q_0, U, F, \Sigma, \{0, 1\}, \delta)$ and input tape x with $l_1(x) = m$ and $l_2(x) = n$ are given. As in the part (3), we assume that it begins to move at the position $(m + 1, n + 1)$, and that when M accepts an input x, it enters an accepting state at the position $(m + 1, n + 1)$ with the marker held in the finite control. For simplicity of the proof, we also assume that if $([q, 1], [a, 0], d) \in \delta([q', 0], [a, 1])$ for some $q, q' \in Q$ and $a \in \Sigma$, then $d =$ stationary, i.e. when M picks up the laid marker from the input tape, its transition is always motionless.

For each $i(0 \le i \le m+1)$, define the mappings

$$f_i^{\uparrow-}, f_i^{\downarrow-}, f_i^{\uparrow+} : Q \times \{0,1,\dots,n+1\} \mapsto \mathcal{P}(\mathcal{P}(Q \times \{0,1,\dots,n+1\}))$$

as follows.

$f_i^{\uparrow-}(q,j) = \{V_1, V_2, \dots, V_K\}$
  $\Leftrightarrow$ there exist K finite computation trees $t_1, t_2, \dots, t_K$ of M on x such that for each $\ell(1 \le \ell \le K)$ (1) the root of t_ℓ is labeled with the configuration $(x^0, [q,0], (i-1,j))$, (2) all internal nodes of t_ℓ are labeled with configurations $(x^0, [q',0], (i',j'))$, where $q' \in Q, j' \in \{0,1,\dots,n+1\}$ and $0 \le i' \le i-1$, and (3) each leaf of t_ℓ is labeled with one of the configurations $(x^0, [q_1,0], (i,j_1)), (x^0, [q_2,0], (i,j_2)), \dots,$ and $(x^0, [q_d,0], (i,j_d))$, where $\{(q_1,j_1), (q_2,j_2), \dots, (q_d,j_d)\} = V_\ell$.
$f_i^{\downarrow-}(q,j) = \{V_1, V_2, \dots, V_K\}$
  $\Leftrightarrow$ There exist K finite computation trees $t_1, t_2, \dots, t_K$ of M on x such that for each $\ell(1 \le \ell \le K)$ (1) the root of t_ℓ is labeled with the configuration $(x_0, [q,0], (i+1,j))$, (2) all internal nodes of t_ℓ are labeled with configurations $(x^0, [q',0], (i',j'))$, where $q' \in Q, j' \in \{0,1,\dots,n+1\}$ and $i+1 \le i' \le m+1$, and (3) each leaf of t_ℓ is labeled with one of the configurations $(x^0, [q_1,0], (i,j_1)), (x^0, [q_2,0], (i,j_2)), \dots,$ and $(x^0, [q_d,0], (i,j_d))$, where $\{(q_1,j_1), (q_2,j_2), \dots, (q_d,j_d)\} = V_\ell$.
$f_i^{\uparrow+}(q,j) = \{V_1, V_2, \dots, V_K\}$
  $\Leftrightarrow$ There exist K finite computation trees $t_1, t_2, \dots, t_K$ of M on x such that for each $\ell(1 \le \ell \le K)$ (1) the root of t_ℓ is labeled with the configuration $(x^0, [q,1], (i-1,j))$, (2) all internal nodes of t_ℓ are labeled with configurations $(x', [q',u'], (i',j'))$, where $q' \in Q, j' \in \{0,1,\dots,n+1\}$ and either (i) $x' = x^0$, $u' = 1$, $0 \le i' \le i-1$ or (ii) $x' = x^{+\langle i'',j''\rangle}$, $u' = 0$, $i' \in \{0,1,\dots,m+1\}$ for some $i'', j''(0 \le i'' \le i-1, 0 \le j'' \le n+1)$, and (3) each leaf of t_ℓ is labeled with one of the configurations $(x^0, [q_1,1], (i,j_1)), (x^0, [q_2,1], (i,j_2)), \dots,$ and $(x^0, [q_d,1], (i,j_d))$, where $\{(q_1,j_1), (q_2,j_2), \dots, (q_d,j_d)\} = V_\ell$.

Since
$$|\mathcal{P}(\mathcal{P}(Q \times \{0,1,\dots,n+1\}))| = 2^{2^{O(n)}},$$

it is clear that, for each i, $O(n) \cdot 2^{O(n)} = 2^{O(n)}$ space suffices in order to record these tables $f_i^{\uparrow+}, f_i^{\uparrow-}$, and $f_i^{\downarrow-}$.

In addition to these mappings, we must use another mapping

$$h_i^- : Q \times \{0,1,\dots,n+1\} \mapsto \mathcal{P}(\mathcal{P}(Q \times \{0,1,\dots,n+1\})),$$

$(0 \le i \le m+1)$ defined as follows:

$h_i^-(q,j) = \{V_1, V_2, \dots, V_K\}$

$\Leftrightarrow$ There exist K finite computation trees $t_1, t_2, \ldots, t_K$ of M on x such that for each $\ell (1 \le \ell \le K)$ (1) the root of t_ℓ is labeled with the configuration $(x^{+\langle i,j \rangle}, [q, 0], (i, j))$, (2) all internal nodes of t_ℓ are labeled with configurations $(x^{+\langle i,j \rangle}, [q', 0], (i', j'))$, where $q' \in Q, i' \in \{0, 1, \ldots, m + 1\}, j' \in \{0, 1, \ldots, n + 1\}$, and (3) each leaf of t_ℓ is labeled with one of the configurations $(x^0, [q_1, 1], (i, j)), (x^0, [q_2, 1], (i, j)), \ldots,$ and $(x^0, [q_d, 1], (i, j))$, where $\{(q_1, j), (q_2, j), \ldots, (q_d, j)\} = V_\ell$.

Intuitively, the elements of $h_i^-(q, j)$ represent the configurations in which M returns to the position (i, j) and picks up the marker again with the assumption that M puts it down previously at the same position in state q.

Now, we describe the main routine which decides the final acceptance or non-acceptance of M on x. Roughly speaking, a 3NT M' performing the procedure acts as follows: While scanning from the top row down to the bottom row of the input, on the ith row M' guesses $f_i^{\downarrow-}$, constructs a) h_i^- from $f_i^{\uparrow-}$ and $f_i^{\downarrow-}$, b) $f_{i+1}^{\uparrow+}$ from $f_i^{\uparrow+}$ and h_i^-, c) $f_{i+1}^{\uparrow-}$ from $f_i^{\uparrow-}$, and checks the validity of $f_{i-1}^{\downarrow-}$. Finally at the $m + 1$st row, M' decides whether or not M accepts x by using the two tables $f_{m+1}^{\uparrow+}$ and h_{m+1}^-.

/* main procedure */
First, set $f_0^{\uparrow-} = \emptyset$ and $f_0^{\uparrow+} = \emptyset$.
For $i = 0$ to $m + 1$ repeat the following (0) through (5):

0) Go to the ith row.
1) Guess $f_i^{\downarrow-}$ arbitrarily, except that when $i = m + 1$ set $f_{m+1}^{\downarrow-} = \emptyset$.
2) To obtain h_i^-, call the subroutine described in Appendix A.
3) [compute $f_{i+1}^{\uparrow+}$ from $f_i^{\uparrow+}$ and h_i^- (for $i \ne m + 1$)]

   For each $(q, j) \in Q \times \{0, 1, \ldots, n+1\}$, do the following to compute $f_{i+1}^{\uparrow+}(q, j)$:
   Initialize a working list $\mathcal{K} = \{\{(q, j)\}\}$;
   If q is an existential state then go to ① else go to ② ;
   Repeat ① and ② below $|Q| \times (n + 2)$ times:
   ① /* processing of existential parts of the computation trees */
        For each set S in $\mathcal{K}$ do the following: Let R be the subset of S each element of which has a check-mark (check-mark indicates the marked element being a configuration which M will enter after going down to the $i + 1$st row). This assures that each element of $S - R$ has an existential state as its first component, or it is a temporary E-element (its meaning shall be explained later). For each $c_\ell = (q', j') \in S - R$ $(1 \le \ell \le |S - R|)$, initialize a working list $H_\ell = \{\}$ and begin to find computation paths of M on x each of whose start nodes is labeled with $(x^0, [q', 1], (i, j'))$ or $(x^0, [q', 1], (i-1, j'))$ if c_ℓ is a temporary E-element $temp_E[(q', j')]$ and whose goal nodes are labeled with some universal configurations or configurations which M will enter just after going down to the $i + 1$st row with the marker held in the finite control. As described in the proof of Theorem 3.3 in Ref. 17, the path search is performed by all the possible one step simulations for unexamined

configurations of M. During the search, if M will go up to the $i-1$st row at the j''th column with the marker held in the finite control and will enter state q'' after that, then refer to the table $f_i^{\uparrow+}$ and continue to search only for the sets in the block corresponding to the pair (q'', j'') that consist of single elements; for any set V of two or more elements, say $V = \{(q_1, j_1), (q_2, j_2), \ldots, (q_d, j_d)\}$ $(d \geq 2)$, add a new type element $temp_U[(q_1, j_1), (q_2, j_2), \ldots, (q_d, j_d)]$, called a *temporary U-element*, to the goal node list H_ℓ. If M would put down the marker at the kth column on the ith row and would enter the state p, then refer to the table $h_i^-(p, k)$ and behave in the same way as the case of its reference to the table $f_i^{\uparrow+}$. When M will enter some universal configuration $(x^0, [q'', 1], (i, j''))$, add the pair (q'', j'') to the list H_ℓ. When M would go down to the $i+1$st row at the j''th column with the marker held in the finite control and would be the state p'' after that, then put a check-mark on (q'', j'') and add the pair to the list H_ℓ. At the end of all path-search, if some goal node list H_ℓ $(1 \leq \ell \leq |S - R|)$ is empty, remove S from $\mathcal{K}$. Finally, insert in $\mathcal{K}$ all sets having the form $\{d_1, d_2, \ldots, d_J\} \cup R$ such that $J = |S - R|$ and $d_\ell \in H_\ell$ for each ℓ $(1 \leq \ell \leq J)$. Remove the old set S from $\mathcal{K}$. Proceed to the next set in $\mathcal{K}$.

② /* processing of universal parts of the computation trees of M */

For each set S in $\mathcal{K}$ do the following: Let R be the subset of S each element of which has a check-mark. (This assures that each element of $S - R$ has a universal state as its first component or is a temporary U-element.) For each $c_\ell = (q', j') \in S - R$ $(1 \leq \ell \leq |S - R|)$, initialize a working list $G_\ell = \{\}$ and begin to perform depth-first search of the computation tree of M whose root is labeled with the configuration $(x^0, [q', 1], (i, j'))$, or if c_ℓ is a temporary U-element $temp_U[(q_1, j_1), (q_2, j_2), \ldots, (q_d, j_d)]$, assume one pseudo-root labeled with a universal configuration whose sons are labeled with $(x^0, [q_1, 1], (i, j_1)), (x^0, [q_2, 1], (i, j_2)), \ldots$, and $(x^0, [q_d, 1], (i, j_d))$. During the search, if it is found that M enters a loop, then stop the search and remove the original S from $\mathcal{K}$. Otherwise, if M will go up to the $i-1$st row at the j''th column with the marker held in the finite control and will enter state q'' after that, then refer to the table $f_i^{\uparrow+}$: if the block corresponding to the pair (q'', j'') has only one set, say $V = \{(q_1, j_1), (q_2, j_2), \ldots, (q_d, j_d)\}$, which means that no existential branch goes out from the configuration $(x^0, [q'', 1], (i-1, j''))$, treat the set V as a U-element $temp_U[(q_1, j_1), (q_2, j_2), \ldots, (q_d, j_d)]$ described above and continue the tree search; if the corresponding block has more than one element, i.e. $V_1, V_2, \ldots, V_K$ $(K \geq 2)$, which means that some existential branch goes out, add a new type element $temp_E[(q'', j'')]$, called a *temporary E-element*, to the corresponding list G_ℓ. If M would put down the marker at the kth column on the ith row and would enter the state p, then refer to the table $h_i^-(p,k)$ and behave in the same way as the case of its reference to the table $f_i^{\uparrow+}$. When M will enter some existential configuration $(x^0, [q'', 1], (i, j''))$, add the pair (q'', j'') to the leaf-node list G_ℓ, and backtrack to its predecessor. When M would go down to the $i+1$st row at the j''th column with the marker held in the finite control and would be the state p'' after that, then put a check-mark on (q'', j'') and add the pair to the list G_ℓ and backtrack to its predecessor.

At the end of all tree-searches for $S - R$, insert in $\mathcal{K}$ the new set $G_1 \cup G_2 \cdots \cup G_J \cup R$, where $J = |S - R|$, and remove the old set S from $\mathcal{K}$. Proceed to the next set in $\mathcal{K}$.

/* final step for construction of $f_{i+1}^{\uparrow+}(q, j)$ */

Copy into $f_{i+1}^{\uparrow+}(q, j)$ the sets $V_1, V_2, \ldots, V_K$ in $\mathcal{K}$, where all elements of V_ℓ ($1 \le \ell \le K$) have check-marks themselves.

Proceed to the next pair in $U \times \{0, 1, \ldots, n+1\}$.

4) Compute $f_{i+1}^{\uparrow-}$ from $f_i^{\uparrow-}$ (for $i \ne m+1$), by the method similar to that of $f_{i+1}^{\uparrow+}$ as shown in 3) above. The details are omitted here.

5) Check the validity of $f_{i-1}^{\downarrow-}$ guessed at the previous row (for $i \ne 0$) by temporally creating a new table $\widehat{f_{-i}^{\downarrow-}}$ from $f_{i-1}^{\downarrow-}$ and checking its equality to the table $f_i^{\downarrow-}$ guessed at the current row. Details are omitted here.

/* decision about the acceptance of M at the bottom boundary row */

Initialize a working list $\mathcal{K} = \{\{(q_0, n+1)\}\}$. Repeat ① and ② above $|Q| \times (n+2)$ times. If there exist a set V in $\mathcal{K}$ such that each pair in V is of the form $(q_f, n+1)$, where $q_f \in F$, then accept x. Otherwise, reject x.

/* end of the main procedure */

It is clear that $T(M') = T(M)$. We next consider the amount of space used by the procedure above. Each description length of the working lists $H_\ell, G_\ell, S - R \subseteq S \in \mathcal{K}$ is at most $2^{O(n)}$. The stack height in step ② is at most $O(n)$. Thus, the total space used by the main procedure is never beyond $2^{O(n)}$. The space required for the subroutine to get h_i^- is also guaranteed below $2^{O(n)}$ (see Appendix A). □

Remark 3.1. In Ref. 2, it is shown that two-way alternating 1-marker automata with n internal states can be simulated by one-way nondeterministic finite automata with $2^{2^{O(n)}}$ internal states. The part (4) of Theorem 3.1 shows an apparent analogy of this, regarding the latter number of internal states as the space bound of our three-way Turing machines.

In the proof of the next lemma, we will refer to a particular two-dimensional automata, named "*two-dimensional on-line tessellation acceptor*" (ota).[5] Intuitively, ota is a kind of rectangular array-bounded cellular space acceptor which is restricted to run in real-time mode in such a way that an anti-diagonal wave of state transition passes diagonally across the cell array once and only once.

Lemma 3.1.

$$(1) \ co\text{-}\mathcal{L}[\text{AF}] \ \subseteq \mathcal{L}[3\text{NT}(n)],$$

$$(2) \ co\text{-}\mathcal{L}[\text{DM1}] \subseteq \mathcal{L}[3\text{NT}(n\log n)],$$

$$(3) \ co\text{-}\mathcal{L}[\text{NM1}] \subseteq \mathcal{L}[3\text{NT}(n^2)],$$

$$(4) \ co\text{-}\mathcal{L}[\text{UM1}] \subseteq \mathcal{L}[3\text{NT}(n^2)],$$

$$(5) \ co\text{-}\mathcal{L}[\text{AM1}] \subseteq \cup_{c>0}\mathcal{L}[3\text{NT}(2^{cn})].$$

Proof. (1): In Ref. 15, it is shown that co–$\mathcal{L}[\text{AF}] \subseteq \mathcal{L}[\text{ota}]$. From this and the other fact $\mathcal{L}[\text{ota}] \subseteq \mathcal{L}[3\text{NT}(n)]$,[5] the relation follows.

(2): It is shown in Theorem 3.1 of Ref. 11 that $\mathcal{L}[\text{DM1}] \subseteq \mathcal{L}[3\text{NT}(n\log n)]$. In the proof, a 3NT M' accepting $T(M)$ was constructed, where M is the given DM1. By careful reading of the context, it is easily seen that the machine M' satisfies the following property: "For any input, only one machine M_d among the machines branched existentially from the original can enter an accepting state q_f when M' accepts the input." Furthermore, from Proposition 2.1, we can assume that, when M' does not accept the input, the decisive machine M_d enters a rejecting state q_r and all the other branching machines enter some halting states which are neither equal to state q_f nor q_r. From these facts, we convert M' to a desired machine M'' by exchanging the accepting state q_f with the rejecting state q_r, and vice versa.

(3)–(5): From Theorem 3.1 and with the same technique as part (2), we can get the desired results. □

Remark 3.2. The part (2) of Lemma 3.1 can be also derived from Theorem 3.1 together with the closure under complementation which will be shown later in Theorem 4.1.

From Lemma 2.1 and Lemma 3.1, we get the main results for this section.

Theorem 3.2.

$$(1) \quad \mathcal{L}[\text{AF}] \subseteq \mathcal{L}[3\text{UT}(n)],$$

$$(2) \ \mathcal{L}[\text{DM1}] \subseteq \mathcal{L}[3\text{UT}(n\log n)],$$

$$(3) \ \mathcal{L}[\text{NM1}] \subseteq \mathcal{L}[3\text{UT}(n^2)],$$

$$(4) \ \mathcal{L}[\text{UM1}] \subseteq \mathcal{L}[3\text{UT}(n^2)],$$

$$(5) \ \mathcal{L}[\text{AM1}] \subseteq \cup_{c>0}\mathcal{L}[3\text{UT}(2^{cn})].$$

4. CLOSURE PROPERTIES

This section will show the main results of this paper. We first summarize closure properties of one-marker automata under Boolean operations.

4.1. Boolean Operations

In Ref. 8, it is shown that one can make any two-dimensional deterministic finite automaton always halt. We can easily generalize this to the case of deterministic multi-marker automata (DMk's) (it is mentioned in Ref. 16 that we can make any "one-dimensional" deterministic "one-marker" automata always halt).

Lemma 4.1. *Any* DMk ($k \geq 0$) *can be converted to the* DMk *that always halts for any input.*

Proof. Let M be a DMk $M = (Q, q_0, \emptyset, F, \Sigma, \{0,1\}, \delta)$ and x be a given input tape for M. We construct another MNk M' accepting the same set as M. Without loss of generality, we assume that when M accepts x, it enters an accepting state at the position $(1,1)$ with the all markers held in the finite control. In the procedure below, M' performs depth-first-search of the computation trees of M whose roots are labeled with some accepting configuration to seek out the leaf labeled with the initial configuration of M. Recall that for any configuration $(\tilde{x}, [q, \mathbf{u}], (i,j))$ of M on x, either ($u_\ell = 0$ and $v_\ell = 1$) or ($u_\ell = 1$ and $v_\ell = 0$) is true for each $\ell (1 \leq \ell \leq k)$, where $\tilde{x}(i,j) = [x(i,j), \mathbf{v}]$.

main program
global var an extended input tape $\tilde{x}$
begin
    for each $q_f \in F$ **do begin**
        move to the position $(1,1)$;
        initialize $\tilde{x} := x^0$;
        $Backward\_Search(q_f, \mathbf{1})$;
    endfor;
    reject and halt
end
procedure $Backward\_Search(q, \mathbf{u})$;
begin
    if $q = q_0$, $\mathbf{u} = \mathbf{1}$, and the current position is $(1,1)$ **then** accept and halt;
    for each $d \in \{$up, down, left, right, stationary$\}$ **do begin**
        move one (or zero) cell to the reversal direction d^{-1} of d;
        read the extended input tape symbol $[a, \mathbf{v}]$ of this cell;
        for each $q' \in Q$, $\mathbf{u}', \mathbf{v}' \in \{0,1\}^k$ such that
                $([q, \mathbf{u}], [a, \mathbf{v}], d) = \delta([q', \mathbf{u}'], [a, \mathbf{v}'])$ **do begin**
        rewrite the extended input symbol $[a, \mathbf{v}]$ to $[a, \mathbf{v}']$;
        $Backward\_Search(q', \mathbf{u}')$;
        rebuild $q, \mathbf{u}, (\mathbf{v}), d$ from $q', \mathbf{u}', a, (\mathbf{v}')$ by using δ;
        restore the extended input symbol $[a, \mathbf{v}]$ for this position
        endfor;
        move back to the direction d
    endfor
end.

Note that M' needs no extra space for backtracking the tree during the whole search. It is clear that M' always halts and $T(M') = T(M)$.   □

From Lemma 4.1, it follows that $\mathcal{L}[\text{DM}k]$ forms Boolean algebra:

Theorem 4.1. $\mathcal{L}[\text{DM}k]$ $(k \geq 0)$ is closed under each Boolean operation.

By using a straightforward technique, such as a serial concatenation of two machines, we get the closure of any class under intersection operation.

Theorem 4.2. For each $X \in \{\text{NM}k, \text{UM}k, \text{AM}k\}$ $(k \geq 0)$, $\mathcal{L}[X]$ is closed under intersection.

Since both nondeterministic multi-marker automaton (NMk) and alternating multi-marker automaton (AMk) have existential states in its own right, it is trivial that the closure under union operation holds for these classes.

Theorem 4.3. For each $X \in \{\text{NM}k, \text{AM}k\}$ $(k \geq 0)$, $\mathcal{L}[X]$ is closed under union.

4.2. Catenation, Cyclic closure, Closure, and Projection Operations

We next investigate the closure properties under the non-Boolean operations defined in Sec. 2.1.

The following is an analogy of the fact that every one-dimensional "two-way" automata language is closed under "reversal operation".[3]

Theorem 4.4. For each $X \in \{\text{DM}k, \text{NM}k, \text{UM}k, \text{AM}k\}$ $(k \geq 0)$, $\mathcal{L}[X]$ is closed under rotation operation.

Corollary 4.1. For each $X \in \{\text{DM}k, \text{NM}k, \text{UM}k, \text{AM}k\}$ $(k \geq 0)$, $\mathcal{L}[X]$ is closed under row catenation (row cyclic closure, row closure) operation iff $\mathcal{L}[X]$ is closed under column catenation (column cyclic closure, column closure) operation.

The remainder of this section contributes to showing that none of $\mathcal{L}[\text{UF}]$, $\mathcal{L}[\text{AF}]$, $\mathcal{L}[\text{DM1}]$, $\mathcal{L}[\text{NM1}]$, $\mathcal{L}[\text{UM1}]$, and $\mathcal{L}[\text{AM1}]$ is closed under such operations as row (column) catenation, row (column) cyclic closure, row (column) closure, and projection operations. The basic tool here is three-way alternating Turing machine with only universal states, which has been investigated in Sec. 3.

First of all, we show that nonclosure of alternating finite automata with only universal states (UFs). This can be proved by the technique similar to the case of nondeterministic finite automata.[4]

Theorem 4.5. $\mathcal{L}[\text{UF}]$ is not closed under row (column) catenation, row (column) cyclic closure, row (column) closure, or projection operation.

Proof. We first consider row catenation operation. Let

$$T = \{x \in \{0,1\}^{2+} \mid \exists\, m \geq 2[l_1(x) = m \text{ and } x[1, *] = x[m, *]]\} \text{ and}$$
$$T' = \{x \in \{0,1\}^{2+} \mid \exists\, m \geq 2[l_1(x) = m \text{ and } \exists\, i(2 \leq i \leq m)[\, x[1, *] = x[i, *]\,]]\}.$$

Then, it is almost clear[4] that $T \in \mathcal{L}[\mathrm{DF}]$. On the other hand, it is shown in Lemma 5.3 of Ref. 11 that $T \ominus \{0,1\}^{2+} = T' \notin \mathcal{L}[\mathrm{UF}]$, which implies the nonclosure of $\mathcal{L}[\mathrm{UF}]$ under row catenation operation.

Next, we consider row cyclic closure operation. Let

$$T'' = \{x \in \{0,1,2\}^{2+} \mid \exists\, m \geq 3[l_1(x) = l_2(x) = m \text{ and}$$
$$\exists\, n(1 \leq n \leq m-1)[x[(1, n+1), (m, m)] \in \{2\}^{2+} \text{ and}$$
$$\exists\, i(2 \leq i \leq m-1)[x[(i+1, 1), (i+1, n)] \in \{2\}^{2+} \text{ and}$$
$$\forall\, r(1 \leq r \leq m, r \neq i+1)[\; x[(r, 1), (r, n)] \in \{0,1\}^{2+}\;]\text{ and}$$
$$x[(1,1),(1,n)] = x[(i,1),(i,n)]\;]]]\}.$$

Then, it is shown in Theorem 3.1 of Ref. 9 that $T'' \in \mathcal{L}[\mathrm{DF}]$. On the other hand, with the same technique as in the proof of Lemma 5.3 in Ref. 13, it is easily seen that $T''^{\mathrm{RC}} \notin \mathcal{L}[\mathrm{UF}]$, which implies the nonclosure of $\mathcal{L}[\mathrm{UF}]$ under row cyclic closure operation.

We next consider row closure operation. Let

$$S = \{x \in \{2\}^{2+} \mid l_1(x) = 1\}, \text{ and}$$
$$H = \{0,1\}^{2+} \ominus S \ominus T.$$

Then, it is obvious that $H \in \mathcal{L}[\mathrm{DF}]$. On the other hand, with a technique similar to the proof of Lemma 5.3 in Ref. 13, it is easily seen that $H^+ = H \cup \{0,1\}^{2+} \ominus (S \ominus T \ominus \{0,1\}^{2+})^+ \ominus S \ominus T = H \cup (\{0,1\}^{2+} \ominus S \ominus T')^+ \ominus S \ominus T \notin \mathcal{L}[\mathrm{UF}]$, which implies the nonclosure of $\mathcal{L}[\mathrm{UF}]$ under row closure operation.

Lastly, we consider projection operation. Let

$$R = \{x \in \{0,1,[2,0],[2,1]\}^{2+} \mid \exists\, m \geq 2[l_1(x) = m \text{ and } \exists\, i(2 \leq i \leq m)[$$
$$x[i, *] \in \{[2,0],[2,1]\}^{2+} \text{ and}$$
$$\forall\, r(1 \leq r \leq m, r \neq i)[\; x[r, *] \in \{0,1\}^{2+}\;] \text{ and}$$
$$\tau(x[1, *]) = \tau(x[i, *])\;]]\},$$

where $\tau : \{0,1,[2,0],[2,1]\} \mapsto \{0,1\}[\tau(0) = 0, \tau(1) = 1, \tau([2,0]) = 0, \tau([2,1]) = 1]$. Then, it is easily seen that $R \in \mathcal{L}[\mathrm{DF}]$. On the other hand, it holds that $\overline{\tau}(R) = T' \notin \mathcal{L}[\mathrm{UF}]$, where $\overline{\tau}$ is the projection extended from the mapping τ. From these facts, it follows that $\mathcal{L}[\mathrm{UF}]$ is not closed under projection operation. The operations in column direction follow from Corollary 4.1.   □

The following lemma plays a key role in the rest of the paper.

Definition 4.1. Let $f : \mathbf{N} \mapsto \mathbf{N}$ be a function and x be a two-dimensional tape with $l_2(x) = n$. For each $j(1 \leq j \leq l_1(x)/f(n))$, we call

$$x[((j-1)f(n)+1, 1), (jf(n), n)]$$

the jth $f(n)$-*block* of x, when $l_1(x)$ is divided by $f(n)$. We simply denote it by $x[block_f(j)]$.

Lemma 4.2. *Let $f : \mathbf{N} \mapsto \mathbf{N}$ be a function. Define*

$$T[f] = \{x \in \{0,1\}^{2+} \mid \exists\, n \geq 1[l_2(x) = n \quad and \quad \exists\, m \geq 2[l_1(x) = f(n) \cdot m \quad and$$
$$\exists\, i,j(1 \leq i,j \leq m, i \neq j)[\, x[block_f(i)] = x[block_f(j)] \,]]]\}.$$

Then, $T[f] \notin \mathcal{L}[3\mathrm{UT}(L(n))]$ if $L(n) = o(2^{f(n) \cdot n})$.

Proof. Suppose there were a $3\mathrm{UT}(L)$ M accepting $T[f]$. For each $n \geq 1$, let

$$R_f(n) = \{y \in \{0,1\}^{2+} \mid l_1(y) = f(n) \text{ and } l_2(y) = n\}, \text{ and}$$
$$V_f(n) = \{x \in \{0,1\}^{2+} \mid l_1(x) = f(n) \cdot 2^{f(n) \cdot n} \text{ and } l_2(x) = n \text{ and}$$
$$\forall\, i,j(1 \leq i,j \leq 2^{f(n) \cdot n}, i \neq j)[\, x[block_f(i)] \neq x[block_f(j)] \,]\}.$$

In other words, the blocks of any tape in $V_f(n)$ is a permutation of the all elements of $R_f(n)$. $V_f(n)$ is a subset of the complement set of $T[f]$ and hence M never accepts any element of $V_f(n)$. Therefore, for each $x \in V_f(n)$, there must be at least one computation path $P_M(x)$ of M on x which never leads to acceptance (we call it a *non-accepting computation path*).

Among the configurations of $P_M(x)$, let $c_k[P_M(x)]$, $1 \leq k \leq 2^{f(n) \cdot n} - 1$, be the configuration just after M leaves from the kth $f(n)$-block of x, i.e. the configuration when M reaches the $k \cdot f(n) + 1$st row of x; if M never reaches the $k \cdot f(n) + 1$st row of x in the path $P_M(x)$, then let $c_k[P_M(x)]$ be *nil*, where '*nil*' is a new symbol.

For each $x \in V_f(n)$ and each $k(1 \leq k \leq 2^{f(n) \cdot n} - 1)$, let

$$BH_k(x) = \{y \in R_f(n) \mid \exists\, i(1 \leq i \leq k)[y = x[block_f(i)]]\}, \text{ and}$$
$$BL_k(x) = R_f(n) - BH_k(x)$$
$$= \{y \in R_f(n) \mid \exists\, i(k+1 \leq i \leq 2^{f(n) \cdot n})[\, y = x[block_f(i)] \,]\}$$

Then, we get the following.

Proposition 4.1. For any $x, y \in V_f(n)$, any non-accepting computation paths $P_M(x)$, $Q_M(y)$ of M, and any $k_1, k_2(1 \leq k_1, k_2 \leq 2^{f(n) \cdot n} - 1)$,
   if $BH_{k_1}(x) \neq BH_{k_2}(y)$, then $c_{k_1}[P_M(x)] \neq c_{k_2}[Q_M(y)]$.

Proof. Suppose $c_{k_1}[P_M(x)] = c_{k_2}[Q_M(y)]$, but $BH_{k_1}(x) \neq BH_{k_2}(y)$. Then, exactly one of the following two statements holds

1) $\exists\, \beta \in R_f(n)[\beta \in BH_{k_1}(x) - BH_{k_2}(y)]$ (hence, $\beta \in BL_{k_2}(y) - BL_{k_1}(x)$),

2) $\exists\, \beta \in R_f(n)[\beta \in BH_{k_2}(y) - BH_{k_1}(x)]$ (hence, $\beta \in BL_{k_1}(x) - BL_{k_2}(y)$).

We consider two tapes z, z':

(i) $z[(1,1), (k_1 \cdot f(n), n)] = x[(1,1), (k_1 \cdot f(n), n)]$ and
      $z[(k_1 \cdot f(n) + 1, 1), (l_1(z), n)] = y[(k_2 \cdot f(n) + 1, 1), (l_1(y), n)];$

(ii) $z'[(1,1), (k_2 \cdot f(n), n)] = y[(1,1), (k_2 \cdot f(n), n)]$ and
      $z'[(k_2 \cdot f(n) + 1, 1), (l_1(z'), n)] = x[(k_1 \cdot f(n) + 1, 1), (l_1(x), n)].$

That is, z (z') is the concatenated tape of the top (bottom) half of x and the bottom (top) half of y. Thus, $BH_{k_1}(z) = BH_{k_1}(x)$, $BL_{k_2}(z) = BL_{k_2}(y)$, $BH_{k_2}(z') = BH_{k_2}(y)$, and $BL_{k_2}(z) = BL_{k_1}(x)$. From this, in Case 1, it holds that $\beta \in BH_{k_1}(z) \cap BL_{k_1}(z)$, and in Case 2 $\beta \in BH_{k_2}(z') \cap BL_{k_2}(z')$. In other words, either z or z' is in $T[f]$. On the other hand, from the hypothesis $c_{k_1}[P_M(x)] = c_{k_2}[Q_M(y)]$, we can easily construct non-accepting computation paths of M for both tapes z and z'. Thus, M accepts neither z nor z', which contradicts our assumption that M accepts $T[f]$. ☐

Proof of Lemma 4.2 (continued). For each $n \geq 1$, let

$$B_f(n) = \{BH_k(x) \mid x \in V_f(n) \text{ and } 1 \leq k \leq 2^{f(n)\cdot n} - 1\}$$
$$= \{A \subseteq R_f(n) \mid A \neq \emptyset \text{ and } A \neq R_f(n)\}$$

and

$$C_f(n) = \{c_k[P_M(x)] \mid x \in V_f(n) \text{ and } P_M(x) \text{ is a non-accepting computation path}$$
$$\text{of } M \text{ on } x \text{ and } 1 \leq k \leq 2^{f(n)\cdot n} - 1\}.$$

Then, it holds that

$$|B_f(n)| = \binom{2^{f(n)\cdot n}}{1} + \binom{2^{f(n)\cdot n}}{2} + \cdots + \binom{2^{f(n)\cdot n}}{2^{f(n)\cdot n} - 1} = 2^{2^{f(n)\cdot n}} - 2$$

and

$$|C_f(n)| \leq s(n+2)L(n)t^{L(n)} + 1,$$

where s is the number of states of the finite control of M and t is the number of symbols of the working tape of M.

Since $L(n) = o(2^{f(n)\cdot n})$, we get $|B_f(n)| > |C_f(n)|$ for large n. For such an n, there must be two tapes $x, y \in V_f(n)$, non-accepting computation paths $P_M(x)$, $Q_M(y)$ of M, and row numbers $k_1, k_2 (1 \leq k_1, k_2 \leq 2^{f(n)\cdot n} - 1)$ such that $BH_{k_1}(x) \neq BH_{k_2}(y)$ and $c_{k_1}[P_M(x)] = c_{k_2}[Q_M(y)]$, which contradicts Proposition 4.1. This completes the proof of Lemma 4.2. ☐

Theorem 4.6. $\mathcal{L}[\text{DM1}], \mathcal{L}[\text{NM1}], \mathcal{L}[\text{UM1}]$, and $\mathcal{L}[\text{AF}]$ are not closed under row (column) catenation, row (column) cyclic closure, row (column) closure, or projection operation.

Proof. First, we consider row catenation and row cyclic closure operations. Define

$$T' = \{x \in \{0,1\}^{2+} \mid \exists\, m \geq 2[l_1(x) = m \text{ and } \exists\, i(2 \leq i \leq m)[\, x[1,*] = x[i,*]\,]]\}$$

as in the proof of Theorem 4.5. Then, it is shown in Lemma 3.2 of Ref. 10 that $T' \in \mathcal{L}[\text{AF}]$ and it is easily seen that $T' \in \mathcal{L}[\text{DM1}]$. On the other hand, from Lemma 4.2 with $f(n) = 1$ and Theorem 3.2, it follows that $\{0,1\}^{2+} \ominus T' = T'^{\text{RC}} = T[1] \notin \mathcal{L}[\text{NM1}] \cup \mathcal{L}[\text{UM1}] \cup \mathcal{L}[\text{AF}]$, which implies the nonclosure of each class under row catenation and row cyclic closure operations.

Next, we consider row closure operation. Let

$$H' = T' \ominus S \ominus \{0,1\}^{2+},$$

where $S = \{x \in \{2\}^{2+} \,|\, l_1(x) = 1\}$ as in the proof of Theorem 4.5. Then, it is easily seen that $H' \in \mathcal{L}[\text{DM1}] \cap \mathcal{L}[\text{AF}]$. On the other hand, with a technique similar to the proof of Lemma 4.2, we can show that $H'^{+} = H' \cup T' \ominus (S \ominus \{0,1\}^{2+} \ominus T')^{+} \ominus S \ominus \{0,1\}^{2+} = H' \cup T' \ominus (S \ominus T[1])^{+} \ominus S \ominus \{0,1\}^{2+} \notin \mathcal{L}[\text{3UT}(o(2^n))]$. From Theorem 3.2, it follows that $H'^{+} \notin \mathcal{L}[\text{NM1}] \cup \mathcal{L}[\text{UM1}] \cup \mathcal{L}[\text{AF}]$, which implies the nonclosure of each class under row closure operation.

Lastly, we consider projection operation. Let

$$R' = \{x \in \{0,1,[2,0],[2,1]\}^{2+} \,|\, \exists\, m \geq 2[l_1(x) = m \text{ and } \exists\, i,j(1 \leq i,j \leq m, i \neq j)$$
$$[x[i,*], x[j,*] \in \{[2,0],[2,1]\}^{2+} \text{ and}$$
$$\forall\, r(1 \leq r \leq m, r \neq i, r \neq j)[x[k,*] \in \{0,1\}^{2+}] \text{ and}$$
$$\tau(x[i,*]) = \tau(x[j,*])\,]]\},$$

where τ is the mapping $\tau : \{0,1,[2,0],[2,1]\} \mapsto \{0,1\}[\tau(0) = 0, \tau(1) = 1, \tau([2,0]) = 0$ and $\tau([2,1]) = 1]$ as in the proof of Theorem 4.5. Then, it is easily seen that $R' \in \mathcal{L}[\text{DM1}] \cap \mathcal{L}[\text{AF}]$. On the other hand, as shown above, it holds that $\bar{\tau}(R') = T[1] \notin \mathcal{L}[\text{NM1}] \cup \mathcal{L}[\text{UM1}] \cup \mathcal{L}[\text{AF}]$, where $\bar{\tau}$ is the projection extended from the mapping τ. This implies the nonclosure of each class under projection operation.

The nonclosures under the operations in column direction follow from Corollary 4.1. □

It is known that $\mathcal{L}[\text{NF}] \subsetneq \mathcal{L}[\text{ota}]^5$ and both $\mathcal{L}[\text{UF}], \mathcal{L}[\text{AF}]$ are incomparable with $\mathcal{L}[\text{ota}]$.[15] But, the relationship between one-marker automata and ota's however had never been known until now. As a corollary of Theorem 4.6 above, we can solve this problem.

Corollary 4.2. Each of $\mathcal{L}[\text{DM1}], \mathcal{L}[\text{NM1}]$, and $\mathcal{L}[\text{UM1}]$ is incomparable with $\mathcal{L}[\text{ota}]$.

Proof. It is shown in Ref. 5 that $\mathcal{L}[\text{ota}] \subseteq \mathcal{L}[\text{3NT}(n)]$ and shown in Ref. 11 that $\mathcal{L}[\text{DM1}] \not\subseteq \mathcal{L}[\text{3NT}(n)]$. Thus, $\mathcal{L}[\text{DM1}] \not\subseteq \mathcal{L}[\text{ota}]$. On the other hand, it is shown in Ref. 5 that $T[1] \in \mathcal{L}[\text{ota}]$ and we have just shown in Lemma 4.2 that $T[1] \notin \mathcal{L}[\text{3UT}(o(2^n))]$. From the relations (3) and (4) in Theorem 3.2, it follows that $T[1] \notin \mathcal{L}[\text{NM1}] \cup \mathcal{L}[\text{UM1}]$. Combining these facts, we get the corollary. □

Remark 4.1. It is conjectured that $\mathcal{L}[\text{ota}]$ and $\mathcal{L}[\text{AM1}]$ are also incomparable to each other, since if $\mathcal{L}[\text{ota}] \subseteq \mathcal{L}[\text{AM1}]$ were true, then it would be the case that nondeterministic and deterministic polynomial time complexity classes are coincident (i.e. $P = NP$).[12]

Finally, we show the nonclosure properties of two-dimensional alternating one-marker automata (AM1s).

Theorem 4.7. $\mathcal{L}[\text{AM1}]$ is not closed under row (column) catenation, row (column) cyclic closure, row (column) closure, or projection operation.

Proof. We first consider row catenation and row cyclic closure operations. Let

$$T'[n] = \{x \in \{0,1\}^{2+} \mid \exists\, m \ge 2[l_1(x) = m \cdot n \text{ and } l_2(x) = n \text{ and}$$
$$\exists\, i(2 \le i \le m)[\, x[block_n(1)] = x[block_n(i)]\,]]\}.$$

Then, it is shown in Ref. 11 that $(T'[n]^{\mathrm{R}})^{\mathrm{R}} \in \mathcal{L}[\mathrm{NM1}]$. Thus from Theorem 4.4, it holds that $T'[n] \in \mathcal{L}[\mathrm{NM1}] \subseteq \mathcal{L}[\mathrm{AM1}]$. On the other hand, from Lemma 4.2 with $f(n) = n$ and Theorem 3.2, it follows that $\{0,1\}^{2+} \ominus T'[n] = T'[n]^{\mathrm{RC}} = T[n] \notin \mathcal{L}[\mathrm{AM1}]$, which implies the nonclosure of $\mathcal{L}[\mathrm{AM1}]$ under row catenation and row cyclic closure operations:

Next, consider row closure operation. Let

$$H'[n] = T'[n] \ominus S \ominus \{0,1\}^{2+},$$

where $S = \{x \in \{2\}^{2+} \mid l_1(x) = 1\}$ as in the proof of Theorem 4.5. Then, it is easily seen that $H'[n] \in \mathcal{L}[\mathrm{AM1}]$. On the other hand, with a technique similar to Lemma 4.2, we can show that $H'[n]^{+} = H'[n] \cup T'[n] \ominus (S \ominus \{0,1\}^{2+} \ominus T'[n])^{+} \ominus S \ominus \{0,1\}^{2+} = H'[n] \cup T'[n] \ominus (S \ominus T[n])^{+} \ominus S \ominus \{0,1\}^{2+} \notin \mathcal{L}[3UT(o(2^{n^2}))]$. From this fact and Theorem 3.2, it follows that $H'[n]^{+} \notin \mathcal{L}[\mathrm{AM1}]$, which implies the nonclosure of $\mathcal{L}[\mathrm{AM1}]$ under row closure operation.

Lastly, we consider projection operation. Let

$$R'[n] = \{x \in \{0,1,[2,0],[2,1]\}^{2+} \mid \exists\, m \ge 2[l_1(x) = m \cdot n \text{ and } l_2(x) = n \text{ and}$$
$$\exists\, i,j(1 \le i,j \le m, i \ne j)$$
$$[x[block_n(i)], x[block_n(j)]] \in \{[2,0],[2,1]\}^{2+} \text{ and}$$
$$\forall\, r(1 \le r \le m, r \ne i, r \ne j)[\, x[block_n(r)] \in \{0,1\}^{2+}\,] \text{ and}$$
$$\tau(x[block_n(i)]) = \tau(x[block_n(j)])\,]]\},$$

where τ is the mapping $\tau : \{0,1,[2,0],[2,1]\} \mapsto \{0,1\}[\,\tau(0) = 0, \tau(1) = 1, \tau([2,0]) = 0$ and $\tau([2,1]) = 1]$ as in the proof of Theorem 4.5. Then, it is easily seen that $R'[n] \in \mathcal{L}[\mathrm{AM1}]$. On the other hand, as shown above, it holds that $\overline{\tau}(R'[n]) = T[n] \notin \mathcal{L}[\mathrm{AM1}]$, where $\overline{\tau}$ is the projection extended from the mapping τ. This implies the nonclosure of $\mathcal{L}[\mathrm{AM1}]$ under projection operation. The nonclosures under the operations in column direction follow from Corollary 4.1. □

5. SUMMARY

Table 1 summarizes the results obtained in this paper, where the symbol "?" indicates the problem unknown at present. It should be noted that the closure under Boolean operations is closely related to the halting property of these machines. That is, the problems will be settled affirmatively, if we could get the original machines always halt.

Table 1. Closure properties of four-way non-storage automata.

Operation	DF	NF	UF	AF	DM1	NM1	UM1	AM1
Intersection	Y†	Y†	Y†	Y†	Y	Y	Y	Y
Union	Y†	Y†	?	Y†	Y	Y	?	Y
Complementation	Y†	?	N†	N†	Y	?	?	?
Catenation‡	N†	N†	N	N	N	N	N	N
Closure‡	N†	N†	N	N	N	N	N	N
Cyclic Closure‡	N†	N†	N	N	N	N	N	N
Projection	N†	N†	N	N	N	N	N	N

†proved in Refs. 4, 6, 9 and 15.
‡holds for both row (vertical) and column (horizontal) directions.

APPENDIX. THE SUB-PROCEDURE USED IN THE PROOF OF THE PART (4) OF THEOREM 3.1.

In the following, we describe a procedure that computes the mapping h_i^- by referring to the two mappings $f_i^{\uparrow-}$ and $f_i^{\downarrow-}$. With no confusion, we use the same variables and notations as in the main procedure described in the proof of the part (4) of Theorem 3.1.

/* procedure that computes h_i^- on the ith row */
For each $(q, j) \in Q \times \{0, 1, \ldots, n+1\}$ do the following:
    Initialize a working list $\mathcal{K} = \{\{(q, j)\}\}$;
    If q is an existential state then go to ① else go to ②;
    Repeat ① and ② below $|Q| \times (n+2)$ times. (Here, we use two types of temporary E-element. First one is the same as in the main routine and the second one is dual to the first):
    ① /* processing of existential parts of the computation trees */
        For each set S in $\mathcal{K}$ do the following: Let R be the subset of S, each element of which has a check-mark (check-mark indicates here the marked element being a configuration which M will enter after picking up the marker again. (This assures that each element of $S - R$ has an existential state as its first component, or it is a temporary E-element.) For each $c_\ell = (q', j') \in S - R$ $(1 \le \ell \le |S - R|)$, initialize a working list $H_\ell = \{\}$ and begin to find computation paths of M on x each of whose start nodes is labeled with $(x^{+\langle i,j \rangle}, [q', 0], (i, j'))$ if c_ℓ is neither type of temporary E-elements or $(x^{+\langle i,j \rangle}, [q', 0], (i-1, j'))$ if c_ℓ is a temporary E-element of the first type $temp_E[(q', j')]$ or $(x^{+\langle i,j \rangle}, [q', 0], (i+1, j'))$ if c_ℓ is a temporary E-element of the second type $temp_{E'}[(q', j')]$ and whose goal nodes are labeled with some universal configurations or configurations which M will enter after picking up the marker again. During the search, if M will go up to the $i - 1$st row or go down to the $i + 1$st row at the j''th column and enter state q'' after that, then refer to the table

$f_i^{\uparrow -}$ or $f_i^{\downarrow -}$, respectively and continue to search only for the sets in the block corresponding to (q'', j'') that consists of single elements; for any set V of two or more elements, say $V = \{(q_1, j_1), (q_2, j_2), \ldots, (q_d, j_d)\}$ $(d \geq 2)$, add a temporary U-element $temp_U[(q_1, j_1), (q_2, j_2), \ldots, (q_d, j_d)]$ to the goal node list H_ℓ. When M will enter some universal configuration $(x^{+\langle i,j \rangle}, [q'', 0], (i, j''))$, add the pair (q'', j'') to the list H_ℓ. When M would pick up the marker again at the position (i, j) and would be the state p'' after that, then put a check-mark on (q'', j) and add the pair to the list H_ℓ.

At the end of all path-searches, if some goal node list H_ℓ $(1 \leq \ell \leq |S - R|)$ is empty, remove S from $\mathcal{K}$. Finally, insert in $\mathcal{K}$ all sets having the form $\{d_1, d_2, \ldots, d_J\} \cup R$ such that $J = |S - R|$ and $d_\ell \in H_\ell$ for each $\ell (1 \leq \ell \leq J)$. Remove the old set S from $\mathcal{K}$. Proceed to the next set in $\mathcal{K}$.

② /* processing of universal parts of the computation trees */

For each set S in $\mathcal{K}$ do the following: Let R be the subset of S each element of which has a check-mark. (This assures that each element of $S - R$ has a universal state as its first component or is a temporary U-element.) For each $c_\ell = (q', j') \in S - R$ $(1 \leq \ell \leq |S - R|)$, initialize a working list $G_\ell = \{\}$ and begin to perform depth-first search of the computation tree of M whose root is labeled with the configuration $(x^{+\langle i,j \rangle}, [q', 0], (i, j'))$, or if c_ℓ is a temporary U-element $temp_U[(q_1, j_1), (q_2, j_2), \ldots, (q_d, j_d)]$, assume one pseudo-root labeled with a universal configuration whose sons are labeled with $(x^{+\langle i,j \rangle}, [q_1, 0], (i, j_1))$, $(x+\langle i, j \rangle [q_2, 0], (i, j_2))$, $\ldots$, and $(x^{+\langle i,j \rangle}, [q_d, 0], (i, j_d))$. During the search, if it is found that M enters a loop, then stop the search and remove the original S from $\mathcal{K}$. Otherwise, if M will enter some existential configuration $(x^{+\langle i,j \rangle}, [q'', 0], (i, j''))$, add the pair (q'', j'') to the leaf-node list G_ℓ, and then backtrack to its predecessor. If M would pick up the marker again at the position (i, j) and would be the state p'' after that, then put a check-mark on (q'', j) and add the pair to the list G_ℓ and backtrack. When M will go up to the $i - 1$st row or go down to the $i + 1$st row at the j''th column and will enter state q'' after that, then refer to the table $f_i^{\uparrow -}$ or $f_i^{\downarrow -}$, respectively: if the block corresponding to (q'', j'') has only one set, say $V = \{(q_1, j_1), (q_2, j_2), \ldots, (q_d, j_d)\}$, which means that no existential branch goes out from the configuration $(x^{+\langle i,j \rangle}, [q'', 0], (i - 1, j''))$ or $(x^{+\langle i,j \rangle}, [q'', 0], (i + 1, j''))$, respectively, treat the set V as a U-element $temp_U[(q_1, j_1), (q_2, j_2), \ldots, (q_d, j_d)]$ described above and continue the tree search; if the corresponding block has more than one sets, i.e. $V_1, V_2, \ldots, V_K$ $(K \geq 2)$, which means that some existential branch goes out, add to the corresponding list G_ℓ a temporary E-element of the first type $temp_E[(q'', j'')]$ or a temporary E-element of the second type $temp_{E'}[(q'', j'')]$, in accordance with the case whether M will go up or go down from the current row.

At the end of all tree-searches for $S - R$, insert in $\mathcal{K}$ the new set $G_1 \cup G_2 \cdots \cup G_J \cup R$, where $J = |S - R|$, and remove the old set S from $\mathcal{K}$. Proceed to the next set in $\mathcal{K}$.

/* final step for construction of $h_i^-(q, j)$ */

Copy into $h_i^-(q, j)$ the sets $V_1, V_2, \ldots, V_K$ in $\mathcal{K}$, where all elements of each V_ℓ $(1 \leq \ell \leq K)$ have check-marks themselves. Proceed to the next pair in the outermost loop.

/* end of the subroutine */

It is clear that the procedure above certainly computes the mapping h_i^- and that the working space used by M' is bounded below $2^{O(n)}$.   □

REFERENCES

1. M. Blum and C. Hewitt, "Automata on a two-dimensional tape", *IEEE Symp. Switching and Automata Theory*, 1967, pp. 155–160.
2. P. Goralcik, A. Goralcikova and V. Koubek, "Alternation with a pebble", *Inf. Process. Lett.* **38** (1991) 7–13.
3. J. E. Hopcroft and J. D. Ullman, *Introduction to Automata Theory, Languages and Computation*, Addison-Wesley, 1979.
4. K. Inoue, A. Nakamura and I. Takanami, "A note on two-dimensional finite automata", *Inf. Process. Lett.* **7**, 1 (1978) 49–52.
5. K. Inoue and I. Takanami, "Some properties of two-dimensional on-line tessellation acceptors", *Inform. Sci.* **13** (1977) 95–121.
6. K. Inoue and I. Takanami, "A note on closure properties of the classes of sets accepted by tape-bounded two-dimensional Turing machines", *Inform. Sci.* **15** (1978) 143–158.
7. K. Inoue and I. Takanami, "Three-way tape-bounded two-dimensional Turing machines", *Inform. Sci.* **17** (1979) 195–220.
8. K. Inoue and I. Takanami, "A survey of two-dimensional automata theory", *Inform. Sci.* **55** (1991) 99–121.
9. K. Inoue, I. Takanami, and A. Nakamura, "Nonclosure properties of nondeterministic two-dimensional finite automata under cyclic closure", *Inform. Sci.* **22** (1980) 45–50.
10. K. Inoue, I. Takanami and H. Taniguchi, "Two-dimensional alternating Turing machines", *Theoret. Comput. Sci.* **27** (1983) 61–83.
11. A. Ito, K. Inoue and I. Takanami, "The simulation of two-dimensional one-marker automata by three-way Turing machines", *Int. J. Pattern Recognition and Artificial Intelligence* **3**, 3 & 4 (1989) 393–404.
12. A. Ito, K. Inoue and I. Takanami, "Complexity of acceptance problems for two-dimensional automata", in *A Perspective in Theoretical Computer Science*, World Scientific, Singapore, 1989, pp. 70–94.
13. A. Ito, K. Inoue, I. Takanami and H. Taniguchi, "Two-dimensional alternating Turing machines with only universal states", *Inform. Contr.* **55**, 1–3 (1982) 193–221.
14. A. Ito, K. Inoue, I. Takanami and Y. Wang, "The effect of inkdots for two-dimensional automata", *Int. J. Pattern Recognition and Artificial Intelligence* **9**, 5 (1995) 777–796.
15. T. Jiang, O. H. Ibarra and H. Wang, "Some results concerning 2-D on-line tessellation acceptors and 2-D alternating finite automata", *Theoret. Comput. Sci.* **125** (1994) 243–257.
16. T. Jiang and B. Ravikumar, "A note on the space complexity of some decision problems for finite automata", *Inf. Process. Lett.* **40** (1991) 25–31.
17. K. Krithivasan and R. Siromonery, "Array automata and operations on array languages", *Int. J. Comput. Math.* **4**, Section A (1974) 3–30.

18. M. L. Minsky and S. A. Papert, *Perceptrons*, Extended Ed., MIT Press, 1988.
19. A. Rosenfeld, *Picture Languages — Formal models for Picture Recognition*, Academic Press, 1979.
20. A. Rosenfeld and R. Siromoney, "Picture languages — a survey", *Language Design* **I** (1993) 229–245.
21. P. S. P. Wang ed., *Array Grammars, Pattern, and Recognizers*, World Scientific, Singapore, 1989.

Akira Ito received the B.E. and M.E. degrees in electronic engineering from Yamaguchi University in 1981 and 1983, respectively, and Ph.D. degree in engineering from Nagoya University in 1992. Since 1983 he has been with Yamaguchi University. He is presently an associate professor in the Faculty of Engineering.

His current interests are automata theory and design of algorithms especially for digital image processing.

Katsushi Inoue received the B.E. and M.E. degrees in electrical engineering from Hiroshima University in 1969 and 1971, respectively, and Ph.D. degree in electrical engineering from Nagoya University in 1977.

From 1971 to 1973, he joined Musashino Electrical Communication Laboratory, NTT, Musashino. Since 1973 he has been with Yamaguchi University. He is presently a professor in the Faculty of Engineering.

His main interests are automata theory, computational geometry and parallel processing.

Yue Wang received his B.E. degree in automatic engineering from Qing-Hua University, China, in 1986, the M.E. degree in information engineering from Yamagata University in 1991, and the Ph.D. degree in system engineering from Yamaguchi University in 1994, respectively. He is presently a lecturer in the Faculty of Engineering, Yamaguchi University.

His research interests include automata theory, computational complexity and parallel processing.

PARALLEL DISTRIBUTED DETECTION OF AN INVARIANT FEATURE ASSOCIATED WITH SELF-SIMILAR PATTERNS

KOHJI KAMEJIMA

Faculty of Engineering, Osaka Institute of Technology
5-16-1 Omiya, Asahi, Osaka 535, Japan
E-mail: GCB01074@niftyserve.or.jp

A parallel distributed scheme is presented for extracting a computable feature associated with self similar patterns. Observed patterns are assumed to be specified in terms of a set of contraction mappings that evokes an "avalanche of exploration" in image field. This intrinsically non-deterministic imaging process yields a conditional probability that is represented on a diffusion system. For identifying mapping set, a parallel projection algorithm is designed on a computable set of local minimums of the conditional distribution. The scheme is applied to dynamic detection of fractal patterns.

Keywords: Invariant feature, parallel distributed scheme, self-similar pattern, diffusion system, pattern coding.

1. INTRODUCTORY REMARKS

Despite continuous deformation, visual information is articulated into a set of "alphabet of patterns" maybe consisting of simple figures[5] or fractal patterns.[6] The articulation of imagery plays a crucial role in various applications including propositional scene analysis.[4,5] In articulating observed imagery, the alphabet should be defined based on the pattern to be generated. By this self reference, articulation process yields explosion of potential decisions. Symbol manipulation schemes enumerate this potential explosion through successive search. A practical approach to image articulation, thus, is the introduction of non-determinism.

Let a "program" be coded in terms of mappings $\mu_i, i = 1, 2, 3, \ldots$ from a bounded image plane $\Omega \subset R^2$ into itself for specifying a sequence of patterns $\{\Xi_t\}$ through explorative expansion:

$$\omega_{t+1} \in \bigcup_{i=1}^{m} \mu_i(\Xi_t), \qquad (1a)$$

where $\Xi_t = \{\omega_\tau \in \Omega, \tau \le t\}$. The imaging process (1a) well generates *ordered-by-results* patterns, if exist, through "avalanche of exploration" triggered by pre-assigned "seeds" $\Xi_0 = \Theta$. By restricting the "programming language" $\{\mu_i\}$ in the class M, the totality of contraction mappings $\Omega \to \Omega$, we can identify the object image Λ with uniquely generated attractor Ξ of the mapping set $\nu = \{\mu_i\}$, i.e.

$$\Lambda \approx \Xi = \lim_{t \to \infty} \Xi_t. \qquad (1b)$$

Parallel Image Analysis: Tools and Models (1998) 29–42

Let the class of "visibles" be restricted to $\mathcal{F} = \mathcal{B}[\Omega]$, the Borel field of subsets of Ω, and define $\mathcal{N} = \mathcal{B}[M]$. Then the generation rule (1) induces an $\mathcal{F}$-measurable coding system $\{M, \mathcal{N}\}$ through the following equivalence:

$$\mathcal{F} \ni \Lambda \approx \Xi \in \mathcal{F} \Longleftrightarrow \nu \in \mathcal{N} . \tag{2}$$

In this paper, a parallel distributed scheme is presented for identifying the imaging process (1) through probabilistic evaluation on $(\Omega, \mathcal{F})$.

2. BASIC CONCEPT AND STATEMENT OF PROBLEM

Define $dP(\omega) = d\omega / \int_{\Omega} d\omega$ and consider the following stochastic version of the pattern detection problem on the probability space $(\Omega, \mathcal{F}, P)$: *Identify the imaging process for generating an image Λ that maximizes the conditional probability*

$$P \left\{ \Lambda \approx \Xi \,\middle|\, \Xi = \bigcup_{\nu} \mu_i(\Xi) \right\} . \tag{3}$$

By assumption (1), this identification problem results in the design of a joint process: *the detection of code ν and the generation of equivalents $\Xi \approx \Lambda$.* Assume that observed image Λ is "sufficiently smooth" in the sense that there exists a infinitely differentiable non-negative function ϕ on Ω with a compact support supp $[\phi]$ in Λ, i.e.

$$\phi(\omega) > 0 \text{ for } \omega \in \text{supp } [\phi] . \tag{4}$$

In addition, assume that observed image Λ is "ordered by ν" so that the following condition is satisfied:

$$\Lambda \cap \mu_i(\Lambda) \neq \emptyset, \text{ for all } \mu_i \in \nu . \tag{5}$$

The function ϕ indicates the domain of mappings $\{\mu_i\}$ and Eq. (5) implies that the "origins" of the imaging process Θ is detectable in a non-empty subset of Λ:

$$\Theta \subset \bigcup_{\nu} [\Lambda \cap \mu_i(\Lambda)] . \tag{6}$$

For such "well visualized" object, the condition $\{\Lambda \approx \Xi = \bigcup_{\nu} \mu_i(\Xi)\}$ in (3) is represented by measurable information $\mathcal{M} = (\Lambda, \Theta, \nu, \phi)$ where

$$\begin{aligned}
\Lambda \in \mathcal{F}; \quad & \text{image of object,} \\
\Theta \in \mathcal{F}; \quad & \text{origin of image,} \\
\nu \in \mathcal{N}; \quad & \text{generator of origins,} \\
\phi \in C_0^{\infty}(\Omega); \quad & \text{indicator of generator.}
\end{aligned}$$

Thus, for well-visualized patterns, the detection of object code ν results in the identification of morphological structure. In what follows, an initial guess is assumed to be given for object codes $\mathcal{V}_0 = \{\nu\}$ and a diffusion system is invoked for parallel estimation $\tilde{\Theta}$ of the origins Θ based on the observation Λ. The condition for sufficient estimation, i.e. $\Theta \in \mathcal{B}[\tilde{\Theta}]$, is obtained via the similarity analysis of the diffusion field. Based on this estimate, a joint iconic-symbolic procedure is implemented for the following successive approximation:

$$\text{supp}[\phi] \to \Lambda, \tag{7a}$$

$$\bigcup_\nu \mu_i(\Theta) \to \Theta, \tag{7b}$$

with initial guess $\mathcal{V}_0$ and $\tilde{\Theta}$.

3. STOCHASTICS IN MORPHOLOGICAL COMPUTATION PROCESS

The morphological structure $\mathcal{M}$ is computable if ϕ is generated based on discrete Θ and finite code ν. For contraction alphabet M, we can define a sub-class of measurable patterns $\Sigma = \{\sigma \mid \sigma \in \mathcal{F}\}$ by

$$\sigma = \left\{ \omega \in \Omega \,\middle|\, \omega \in \bigcup_\nu \mu_i(\Omega) \right\}, \quad \nu \in \mathcal{N}. \tag{8}$$

By the σ-additivity of the class $\mathcal{N}$, the morphological event $\sigma \in \Sigma$ is also measurable. This implies that the similarity between a testing pattern $\sigma \in \mathcal{F}$ and observed patterns with morphological structure $\mathcal{M} = (\Lambda, \Theta, \nu, \phi)$ is evaluated by the conditional probability. Define $P(\sigma \mid \mathcal{M})$ by

$$P(\sigma \mid \mathcal{M}) = \int_\sigma p(\omega \mid \Lambda) dP(\omega), \tag{9a}$$

$$p(\omega \mid \Lambda) = \varphi(\omega) / \int_\Lambda \varphi(\omega) d\omega. \tag{9b}$$

where φ denotes the solution to the following Dirichlet problem:

$$\Delta\varphi(\omega) = \rho\varphi(\omega), \rho > 0, \omega \in \Lambda, \tag{10a}$$

$$\varphi(\omega) = 0, \omega \in \Omega - \bar{\Lambda}, \tag{10b}$$

$$\varphi(\omega') = 1, \omega' \in \partial\Lambda. \tag{10c}$$

Since $\Delta p(\omega \mid \Lambda) \geq 0$, a.e. in Λ, by (10), the conditional distribution $p(\omega \mid \Lambda)$ is subharmonic in Λ, i.e.

$$0 \leq p(\omega \in \sigma \mid \Lambda) \leq p(\omega \in \Lambda \mid \Lambda) < \infty, \text{ a.e.} \tag{11}$$

Thus, we have a version of conditional probability $P(\sigma \mid \mathcal{M})$ with the following properties:

$$0 \leq P(\sigma \mid \Lambda) \leq P(\Lambda \mid \Lambda) = 1, \text{ for } \sigma \in \Sigma, \Lambda \in \mathcal{F}, \tag{12a}$$

$$P(\cup\sigma_i \mid \Lambda) = \sum_i P(\sigma_i \mid \Lambda), \text{ for } \sigma_i \in \Sigma, \sigma_i \cap \sigma_j = \emptyset, \tag{12b}$$

$$P(\sigma \mid \cup\Lambda_i) = \sum_i P(\sigma \mid \Lambda_i)\delta P, \text{ for } \Lambda_i \in \mathcal{F}, \Lambda_i \cap \Lambda_j = \emptyset, P(\Lambda_i) = P(\Lambda_j), \tag{12c}$$

where $\delta P = P(\Lambda_i)/P(\cup \Lambda_i)$. From the maximum principle (11), we have a discrete set $\Theta_\Lambda^0 = \{\theta \in \Lambda \mid p(\theta \mid \Lambda) \leq p(\omega \in \Lambda \mid \Lambda)\}$. This feature pattern Θ_Λ^0 is a stochastic extension of the location.

The stochastic evaluation (9) can also be applied to the similarity analysis of a "static" pattern generation process. Let $\Lambda \in \mathcal{F}$ be a fixed observation pattern and suppose that $\nu^0 = \{\mu_i^0 \in M\}$ is a fixed set of contraction mappings satisfying the following "separation" condition:

$$\Lambda_i \cap \Lambda_j = \emptyset, \text{ for } i \neq j, \tag{13}$$

where $\Lambda_i = \mu_i^0(\Lambda)$. Define a mapping $\tilde{\mu}_i$ by

$$\tilde{\mu}_i(\omega) = \omega, \text{ for } \omega \in \Lambda_i, \tag{14a}$$

$$P\{\tilde{\mu}_i(\omega) \mid \omega \in \Omega - \Lambda_i\} = 0, \tag{14b}$$

for each μ_i^0. Then we have a non-expansive projector $\tilde{\nu}[\nu^0] = \{\tilde{\mu}_i\}$ induced by contraction mappings ν^0. Define $\Xi^0 = \bigcup_{\nu^0} \Lambda_i$. Since $\Xi_0 = \{\omega \in \bigcup_{\nu^0} \Lambda_i \mid \omega \in \bigcup_{\tilde{\nu}} \tilde{\mu}_i(\Xi^0)\}$, the projector $\tilde{\nu}$ can be identified with the invariant set Ξ^0. In addition, we have a trivial invariant feature associated with a mapping class $\tilde{\nu}$:

$$\Theta^0 = \left\{ \theta \in \bigcup_{\nu^0} \Theta_{\Lambda_i}^0 \,\middle|\, \theta \in \bigcup_{\tilde{\nu}} \tilde{\mu}_i(\Theta^0) \right\}, \tag{15}$$

where $\Theta_{\Lambda_i}^0 = \{\theta_i \in \bigcup_{\nu^0} \Lambda_i \mid p(\theta_i \mid \Lambda_i) \leq p(\omega \in \Lambda_i \mid \Lambda_i)\}$. Thus, for any morphological events with trivial self-similarity $\Xi^0 = \{\omega \in \Omega \mid \omega \in \bigcup_{\tilde{\nu}} \tilde{\mu}_i(\Xi^0)\}$, we can extend the stochastic evaluation by the following conditional probability:

$$P(\sigma \mid \mathcal{M}^0) = \int_\sigma p(\omega \mid \Xi^0)d\omega, \quad 0 \leq p(\omega \mid \Xi^0) < \infty, \text{ a.e.}, \tag{16}$$

where $\mathcal{M}^0 = (\Xi^0 \in \mathcal{F}, \Theta^0 \in \mathcal{F}, \nu^0 \in \mathcal{N}, \phi \in C_0^\infty(\Xi^0))$.

4. EXTENSION TO SELF-SIMILAR PATTERNS

As shown in Eq. (15), the projector $\tilde{\nu}[\nu^0]$ generates invariant feature Θ^0 through no explicit interaction with the invariant set Ξ^0. Thus we can specify the code ν^0, that generates Ξ^0, based on computable information Θ^0. This computability can be extended to generalized invariant sets. Let $\nu = \{\mu_i\}$ be a contraction mapping satisfying the following open set condition[3]

$$\bigcup_\nu \mu_i(O) \subset O, \tag{17a}$$

$$\mu_i(O) \cap \mu_j(O) = \emptyset \text{ for any } \mu_i, \mu_j \in \nu, \tag{17b}$$

and suppose that Ξ is associated invariant set:

$$\Xi = \{\omega \in \Omega \mid \omega \in \bigcup_\nu \mu_i(\Xi)\}. \tag{18}$$

Define "slightly smoothed region" by

$$\Xi^\epsilon = \left\{ \omega \in \Omega \,\middle|\, \int_\Omega \left(\frac{1}{\epsilon^2}\right) m \left(\frac{\omega - \xi}{\epsilon}\right) d\chi[\Xi](\xi) > 0 \right\}, \tag{19}$$

where $\chi[\cdot]$ is the invariant measure associated with attractor $(\cdot)^2$ and $m \in C_0^\infty(\Omega)$ denotes a mollifier of fractal region Ξ. Then, in observables $\tilde{\Theta} = \{\tilde{\theta} \in \Xi^\epsilon \mid \nabla p(\tilde{\theta} \mid \Xi^\epsilon) = 0, p(\tilde{\theta} \mid \Xi^\epsilon) > 0\}$, we can specify the sufficient condition for the existence of an invariant feature associated with ν:

$$\Theta = \left\{ \theta \in \tilde{\Theta} \,\middle|\, \theta \in \bigcup_\nu \mu_i(\Theta) \right\}. \tag{20}$$

Equation (18) combined with Eq. (20) implies that the object with image Ξ is well coded into ν via computational process on $\tilde{\Theta}$. Thus, for any morphological events associated with self-similar mappings $\nu = \{\mu_i\}$, we have the following conditional probability:

$$P(\sigma \mid \mathcal{M}) = \int_\sigma p(\omega \mid \Xi^\epsilon) d\omega, \quad 0 \le p(\omega \mid \Xi^\epsilon) < \infty, \text{ a.e.}, \tag{21}$$

where $\mathcal{M} = (\Xi \in \mathcal{F}, \Theta \in \mathcal{F}, \nu \in \mathcal{N}, \phi \in C_0^\infty(\Xi^\epsilon))$. The definition of conditional distribution combined with the description of feature pattern implies that an estimate of the invariant set Θ is detected through a parallel distributed scheme (see Fig. 1).

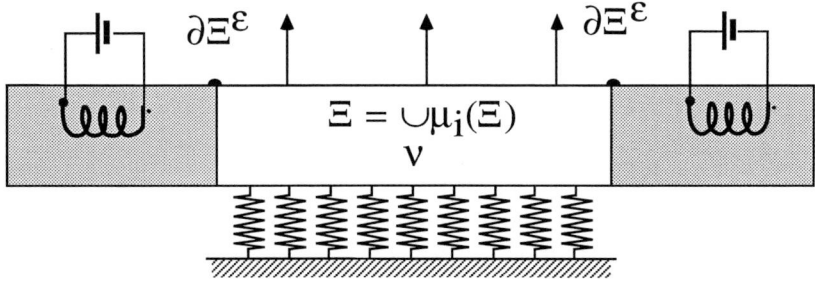

Fig. 1.   Feature pattern detector.

5. EXISTENCE OF INVARIANT FEATURE

By a set of contraction mappings $\nu = \{\mu_i\}$, the observables $\tilde{\Theta}$ is transferred into Ξ. However, the distribution $p(\omega \mid \Xi_i)$ is not identical with the restriction of $p(\omega \mid \Xi^\epsilon) \approx \varphi(\omega)$ to Ξ_i due to the disparity of boundary condition (Fig. 2). In this section, the trajectory of observables $\tilde{\Theta}$ through a "boundary preserving contraction process" is analyzed.

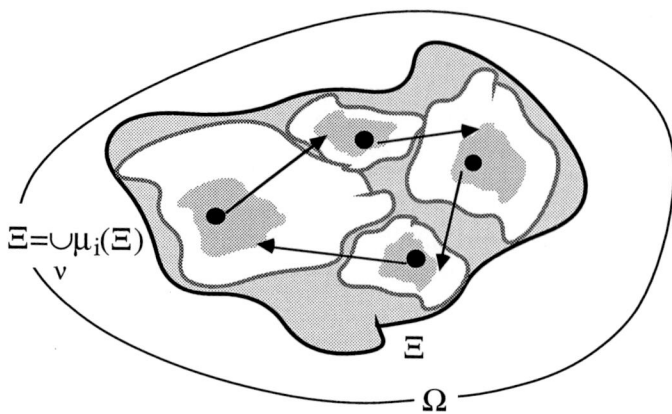

Fig. 2.   Existence of invariant feature.

First, noting that the continuity of distribution φ is preserved through continuous mapping, we have

Proposition 1 *Let μ be a contraction mapping of Ξ^ϵ into itself and suppose that $\tilde{\Theta}_\mu = \{\tilde{\theta} \in \Xi_\mu \mid \nabla\varphi_\mu = 0, \varphi_\mu > 0\}$, is feature points associated with reduced region $\Xi_\mu = \mu(\Xi^\epsilon)$, where*

$$\Delta\varphi_\mu(\omega) = \rho\varphi_\mu(\omega), \quad \omega \in \Xi_\mu, \tag{22a}$$

$$\varphi_\mu(\omega) = 0, \quad \omega \in \Omega - \bar{\Xi}_\mu, \tag{22b}$$

$$\varphi_\mu(\omega') = 1, \quad \omega' \in \mu(\partial\Xi_\mu). \tag{22c}$$

Then $\tilde{\Theta}_\mu \subset \mu(\tilde{\Theta}) \subset \Xi_\mu$.

For tracing the trajectory under boundary preserving contractions, define $\partial_i = \mu_i(\partial\Xi^\epsilon)$ and consider the solution $\{\varphi_i, i = 1, 2, \ldots\}$ to the following system:

$$\Delta\varphi_i(\omega) = \rho\varphi_i(\omega), \quad \omega \in \Xi_i = \mu_i(\Xi^\epsilon), \tag{23a}$$

$$\varphi_i(\omega) = 0, \quad \omega \in \Omega - \bar{\Xi}_i, \tag{23b}$$

$$\varphi_i(\omega') = 1, \quad \omega' \in \partial_i = \mu_i(\partial\Xi^\epsilon). \tag{23c}$$

By Proposition 1, the system (23) maps the set Ξ^ϵ with its boundary $\partial\Xi^\epsilon$. Let the map of feature distribution $\mu(\tilde{\Theta})$ be transferred through continuation process (Fig. 3). In this process, the boundary value $\varphi_i(\omega')$ is smoothly changed to the value of associated field $\varphi(\omega')$. By this operation, we have the trajectory of feature patterns as follows:

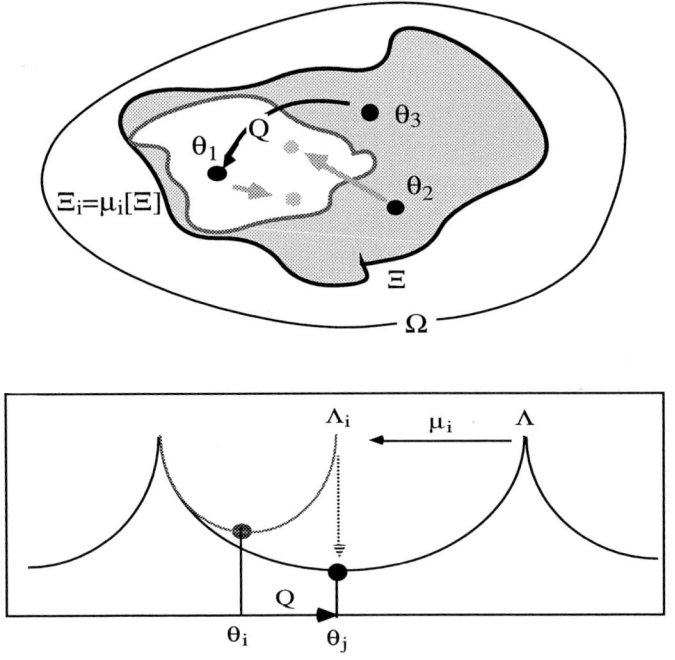

Fig. 3. Continuation process associated with self-similar mappings.

Proposition 2 *Define the one parameter group of distributions* $\varphi^\alpha : \alpha \in [0,1]$ *by*

$$\Delta\varphi^\alpha(\omega) = \rho\varphi^\alpha(\omega), \quad \omega \in \Xi^\epsilon - \bigcup_\nu \partial_i, \tag{24a}$$

$$\varphi^\alpha(\omega^\circ) = (1-\alpha) + \alpha\varphi(\omega^\circ), \quad \omega^\circ \in \bigcup_\nu \partial_i \subset \Xi^\epsilon, \tag{24b}$$

$$\varphi^\alpha(\omega) = 0, \quad \omega \in \Omega - \bar{\Xi}^\epsilon, \tag{24c}$$

$$\varphi^\alpha(\omega') = 1, \quad \omega' \in \partial\Xi^\epsilon. \tag{24d}$$

Assume that there exists a curve Q *consisting of points* $\tilde{\theta}^\alpha$, $0 \le \alpha \le 1$ *satisfying the following differential equation:*

$$\frac{d\tilde{\theta}^\alpha}{d\alpha} = -\left[\nabla\nabla^T\varphi^\alpha\right]^{-1}\frac{\partial\nabla\varphi^\alpha}{\partial\alpha}, \quad 0 \le \alpha \le 1, \tag{25}$$

with boundary condition $\tilde{\theta}^0 \in \bigcup_\nu \mu_i(\tilde{\Theta})$ *and* $\tilde{\theta}^1 \in \tilde{\Theta}$. *Then the feature point* $\tilde{\theta}^\alpha$, $0 \le \alpha \le 1$, *lies in a curve* Q.

Proof. By definition,

$$\varphi^\alpha(\omega) : \varphi_i(\omega) \to \varphi(\omega) \text{ for } \alpha : 0 \to 1 \text{ and } \omega \in \Xi_i. \tag{26}$$

Let $\tilde{\theta}^\alpha : \nabla\varphi^\alpha(\tilde{\theta}^\alpha) = 0$. Since $\varphi(\tilde{\theta}^\alpha)$ is uniformly continuous in Ξ^ϵ, the solution to the differential equation (25) is unique. Noticing the maximality of the feature points $\tilde{\Theta}$, i.e.

$$\nabla\varphi_i \neq 0 \text{ for any } \omega \in \Omega - \bigcup_\nu \tilde{\Theta}_i, \tag{27}$$

and $\tilde{\theta}^0 \in \bigcup_\nu \tilde{\Theta}_i$, we have the trajectory $\tilde{\Theta}^\alpha = \{\tilde{\theta}^\alpha \in \Xi^\epsilon \cap Q \mid \nabla\varphi^\alpha = 0\}$, with $\tilde{\Theta}^1 = \tilde{\Theta}$. $\square$

Generally, the path governed by (25) is not ensured to connect observables $\tilde{\Theta}$. However, in well-ordered patterns satisfying condition (5), we can select a set of feature points invariant with respect to mappings ν. The sufficient condition for the existence of invariant feature is specified in the following.

Theorem 3 *Suppose that the code ν generates an invariant set $\bigcup_\nu \mu_i(\Xi) = \Xi$ and assume that the observation $\tilde{\Theta} = \{\tilde{\theta} \in \Xi^\epsilon \mid \nabla p(\tilde{\theta} \mid \Xi^\epsilon) = 0, p(\tilde{\theta} \mid \Xi^\epsilon) > 0\}$ is sufficient in the following sense:*

$$\tilde{\Theta} \cap [\Xi^\epsilon - \Xi] = \emptyset \quad and \quad \left[\bigcup_\nu \mu_i(\tilde{\Theta})\right] \cap \tilde{\Theta} \neq \emptyset. \tag{28}$$

Then, there exists an invariant feature $\Theta = \{\theta \in \tilde{\Theta} \mid \theta \in \bigcup_\nu \mu_i(\Theta)\}$ in $\tilde{\Theta}$.

Proof. Define $\hat{\Theta} = \left[\bigcup_\nu \mu_i(\tilde{\Theta})\right] \cap \tilde{\Theta}$. By sufficiency (28), there exists a trajectory with origin $\tilde{\theta}_0$ in $\tilde{\Theta}$ and destination $\tilde{\theta}_1$ in $\hat{\Theta}$. Noticing the continuity of the path governed by (25), the condition $\hat{\Theta} \neq \emptyset$ implies that the distance between mapped feature point $\tilde{\theta}^0 = \tilde{\theta}_1$ and moved point $\tilde{\theta}^1$ is negligible. Since $\tilde{\Theta} \subset \Xi$ and $\tilde{\theta}_1 \in \hat{\Theta}$, Proposition 1 implies that the origin $\tilde{\theta}_0 \in \tilde{\Theta}$ must be generated in the mapping image of $\tilde{\Theta}$. Hence, $\tilde{\theta}^0 \in \hat{\Theta}$, i.e. the set of destinations $\hat{\Theta}$ contains all origins of itself, as was to be proved. $\square$

Furthermore, by selecting effective mappings in detected code ν, we have a self-similar pattern in observed image Λ, i.e.

Theorem 4 *Assume that the code $\nu = \{\mu_i\}$, $\mu_i : \Lambda \to \Lambda$ effectively generates an invariant feature*

$$\Theta = \left\{\theta \in \tilde{\Theta} \mid \theta \in \bigcup_\nu \mu_i(\Theta)\right\}, \tag{29a}$$

$$\Theta \cap \mu_i(\Theta) \neq \emptyset, \text{ for all } \mu_i \in \nu, \tag{29b}$$

in observables $\tilde{\Theta} = \{\tilde{\theta} \in \Lambda \mid \nabla\varphi(\tilde{\theta}) = 0, \varphi(\tilde{\theta}) > 0\}$. Then there exists an invariant extension Ξ of Θ in Λ satisfying the following condition:

$$\Theta \subset \Xi = \bigcup_\nu \mu_i(\Xi) \subset \Lambda. \tag{30}$$

Proof. Define a monotone sequence $\hat{\Theta}_{t+1} = \bigcup_\nu \mu_i(\hat{\Theta}_t)$, $\hat{\Theta}_0 = \Theta$. Then, we have $\Theta \subset \hat{\Theta}_t$ and $\hat{\Theta}_t \subset \Lambda$, for all $t \geq 0$. Thus there exists a limit point $\lim_{t \to \infty} \hat{\Theta}_t = \Xi$ in Ξ. The uniqueness of limit point implies that $\Theta \subset \Xi \subset \Lambda$, as was to be proved. □

6. DYNAMIC CODING SCHEME

Consider a parallel distributed implementation of coding scheme (7). The basic idea is to introduce dynamics in the representation of conditional distribution φ. By approximating the solution to (10) a diffusion system, we have a dynamical system for evaluating the conditional probability $P(\omega \mid \mathcal{M})$ associated with observed pattern Λ as follows:

$$\frac{\partial \varphi}{\partial t} = \Delta \varphi - \rho \varphi, \tag{31a}$$

$$\varphi - \chi[\partial \Lambda] \in C_0^\infty(\Lambda). \tag{31b}$$

Considering fractal singularity of attractor Λ, rough constraint[7] $\varphi - \chi[\partial \Lambda] \in C_0^\infty(\Lambda)$ is substituted for exact boundary condition (10c). Based on this field information, the feature pattern is obtained through distributed processing that exploits only local information of φ, i.e.

$$\tilde{\Theta} = \{\tilde{\theta} \in \Omega \mid \nabla \varphi(\tilde{\theta}) = 0, \varphi(\tilde{\theta}) > 0\}. \tag{32}$$

Letting $\Theta_0 = \tilde{\Theta}$ and selecting $\mathcal{V}_0 = \{\nu \in \mathcal{N} \mid \mu(\tilde{\Theta}) \subset \tilde{\Theta}, \mu \in \nu\}$, we have joint computation scheme for successively updating the estimates $\Theta_{\tau+1}$ and $\mathcal{V}_{\tau+1}$:

$$\Theta_{\tau+1} = \left\{ \mu(\theta) \in \tilde{\Theta} \;\middle|\; \theta \in \Theta_\tau, \mu \in \bigcup_{\mathcal{V}_\tau} \nu \right\}, \tag{33a}$$

$$\mathcal{V}_{\tau+1} = \left\{ \nu \in \mathcal{V}_\tau \;\middle|\; \mu(\Theta_\tau) \subset \Theta_\tau, \mu \in \nu \right\}. \tag{33b}$$

This algorithm monotonically reduces the sets $\{\Theta_\tau, \mathcal{V}_\tau\}$ via parallel projection (Fig. 4). The domain of mappings in the class $\{\mathcal{V}_\tau\}$ can be estimated by the following trivial contraction mappings:

$$\tilde{\mu}_{\omega'} : \omega \to \frac{1}{2}(\omega + \omega'), \quad \omega' \in \Lambda, \omega \in \Omega. \tag{34}$$

The iteration of mappings $\{\tilde{\mu}_{\omega'}\}$ yields a sequence of sets $\{\sigma_\tau\}$ that successively approximate the supports of the indicator ϕ associated with mappings $\mu \in \nu$ where $\nu \in \{\mathcal{V}_\tau\}$. Noticing $\bigcup_{\omega' \in \Lambda} \tilde{\mu}_{\omega'}(\Lambda) = \Lambda$, the sequence $\{\sigma_\tau\}$ with initial value $\tilde{\Theta}$ converges to the region Λ. The mapping system $\nu' = \{\tilde{\mu}_{\omega'}\}$ is well simulated by the diffusion system

$$\frac{\partial \phi}{\partial t} = \Delta \phi - \rho \phi, \tag{35a}$$

$$\phi - \chi[\partial \tilde{\Xi}] \in C_0^\infty(\Omega - \tilde{\Xi}), \tag{35b}$$

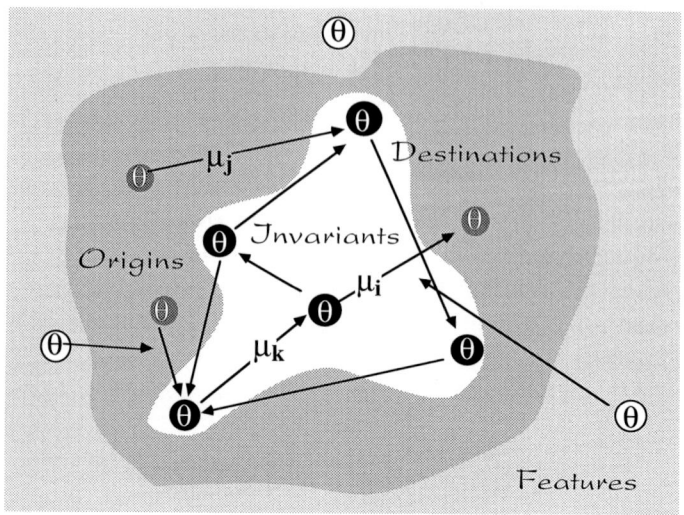

Fig. 4. Invariant feature computation.

where $\tilde{\Xi}$ is determined by the following point wise decision:

$$\tilde{\Xi} = \tilde{\Theta} \cup \{\xi \in \Omega \mid \phi(\xi) \geq \varphi(\xi) > 0, \mid \nabla\varphi(\xi) \mid > 0, \mid \nabla\phi(\xi) \mid > 0\}. \qquad (36)$$

By definition (36), the parallel distributed system (35) generates a sequence of $\mathcal{F}$-measurable sets $\tilde{\Xi}$ that converge to the domain Λ.

Thus, the dynamical system (31)–(36) yields a parallel distributed scheme for coding self-similar patterns. The detector extracts origins Θ in computable information $\tilde{\Theta}$ through coding by ν as well as estimates of image $\tilde{\Xi}$ based on distribution ϕ.

7. EXPERIMENTS

The coding scheme was verified through simulation studies. Patterns to be observed are generated through a Monte Carlo simulation[1] and identified within a preassigned set of attractors, called the dictionary. An example of observed pattern, a version of "Barnsley's Fern", is shown in Fig. 5 and the dictionary is illustrated in Fig. 6. These dictionary patterns are generated based on the set of contraction mappings of the following form: **((REDUCTION** *reduction*)**(ROTATION** *rotation*)**(FLIP** *flip-horizontal*)**(U** *horizontal-shift*)**(V** *vertical-shift*)**)**.

The simulation results are illustrated in Figs. 7 and 8 where a fractal pattern and a composition of fractal patterns are detected through imaging process identification, respectively. In these figures, given pattern Λ and extracted feature points $\tilde{\Theta}$ are shown with associated distributions φ and ϕ in (a). As well, identified code $\nu = \{\mu\}$ is indicated on associated attractor $\Xi = \bigcup_{\nu} \mu_i(\Xi)$ with and estimated

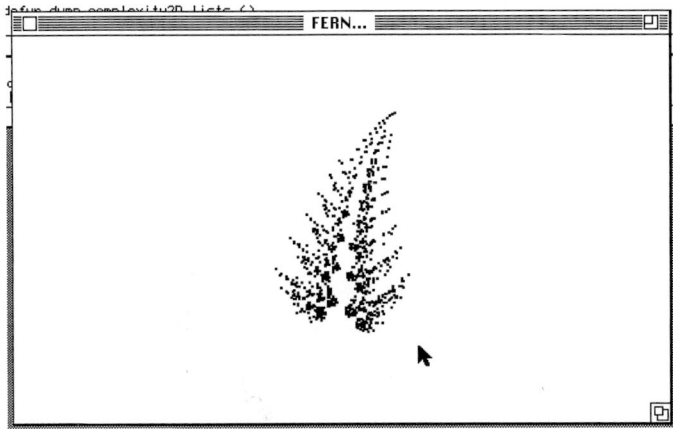

Fig. 5. Pattern to be detected.

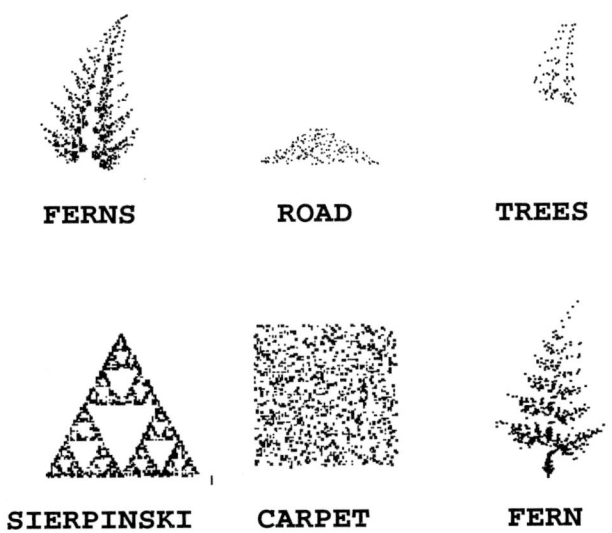

FERNS **ROAD** **TREES**

SIERPINSKI **CARPET** **FERN**

Fig. 6. Dictionary of patterns.

region $\tilde{\Xi}$, in (a). For visualizing identified code, invariant subsets Θ connected by mapping set ν are indicated on regions specified by associated attractor Ξ. Simultaneously, the time evolutions of detection processes are shown in (b) where numbers of points in sets $\tilde{\Theta}$ and $\tilde{\Xi}$ are compared. As shown in (b), the detection of feature points $\tilde{\Theta}$ is completed considerably prior to the regeneration of the estimate $\tilde{\Xi}$. This implies that proposed coding method can identify mapping set ν based on partial restoration of geometric feature, such as region and contours.

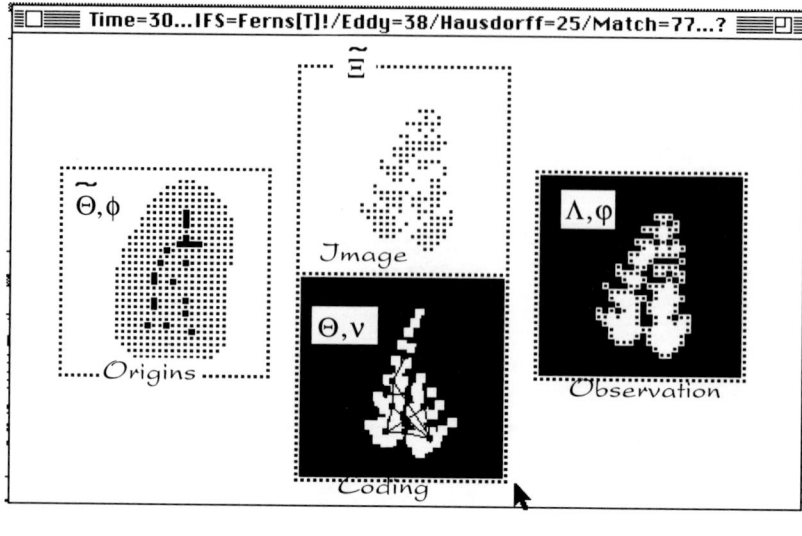

(a)

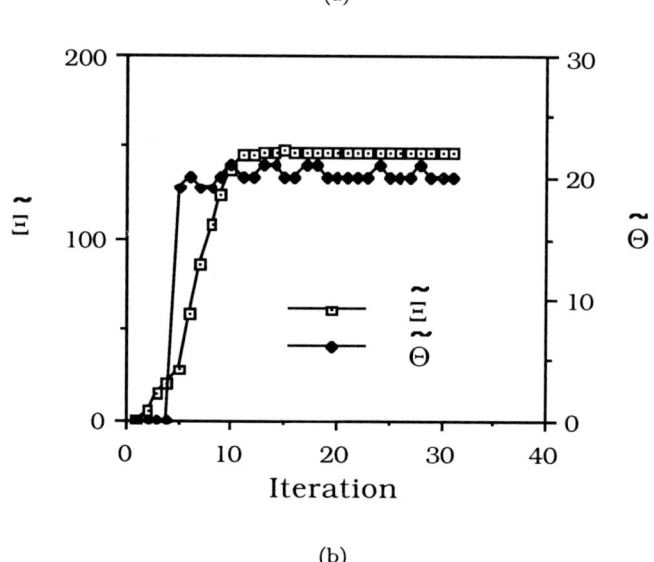

(b)

Fig. 7. Coding of a fractal pattern (a) coding results (b) $\tilde{\Theta}$ vs. $\tilde{\Xi}$.

8. CONCLUDING REMARKS

A conditional probability was introduced for stochastic evaluation of self-similar patterns. By this conditional probability, intrinsically stochastic imaging process is associated with observed patterns. The self-similar mappings are demonstrated to yield invariant computable set specified in feature points of the conditional probability. By representing the conditional probability on a diffusion system, a parallel

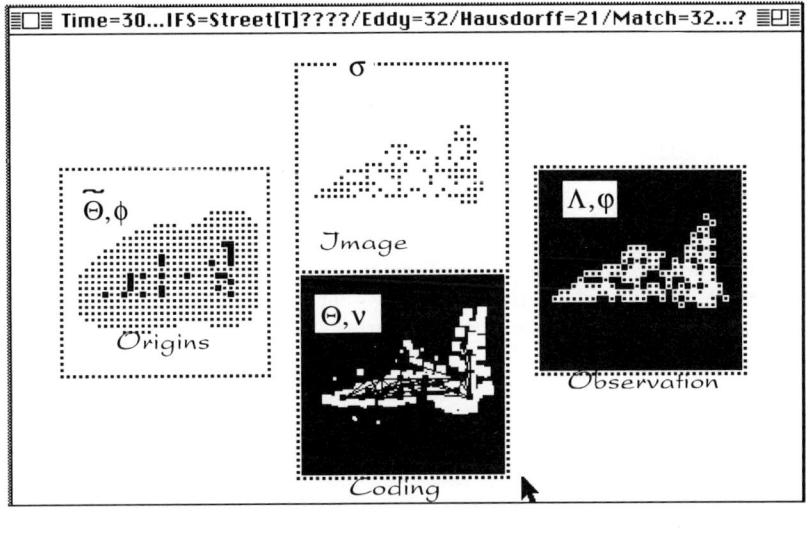

(a)

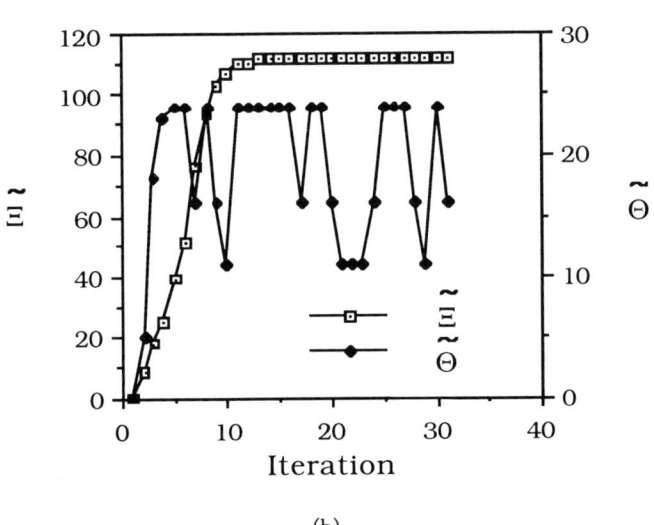

(b)

Fig. 8. Coding of composed patterns (a) coding results (b) $\tilde{\Theta}$ vs. $\tilde{\Xi}$.

projection scheme was introduced for successive detection of invariant features. The detection scheme was applied to the identification of contraction mappings associated with fractal patterns successfully.

REFERENCES

1. M. F. Barnsley, *Fractals Everywhere*, Academic Press, San Diego, 1988.
2. I. Fujita, K. Tanaka, M. Ito and K. Cheng, "Columns for visual features of objects in monkey inferotemporal cortex", *Nature* **360** (1992) 343–346.

3. J. E. Hutchinson, "Fractals and self similarity", *Indiana Univ. Math. J.* **30** (1981) 713–747.

4. K. Kamejima, T. Hamada, M. Tsuchiya and Y. C. Watanabe, "From self navigation to driver's associate: An application of mobile robot vision to a vehicle information system", in *Vision-based Vehicle Guidance*, ed. I. Masaki, Springer-Verlag, New York, 1992, pp. 173–203.

5. K. Kamejima, Y. C. Watanabe and Y. Ichikawa, "Intention, computation and environmental complexity", in *Proc. 2nd Japan–France Congress On Mechatronics*, Takamatsu, 1994, pp. 739–742.

6. Y. Miyashita and H. S. Chang, "Neural correlate of pictorial short-term memory in the primate temporal cortex", *Nature* **331** (1988) 568–570.

7. K. Yosida, *Functional Analysis*, Springer-Verlag, Berlin, 1968.

 **Kohji Kamejima** received his B.E. and M.Sc. degrees in mechanical engineering from Kyoto Institute of Technology in 1971 and 1973, respectively. In 1991, he received his Ph.D. in applied mathematics and physics from Kyoto University.

From 1973 to 1994, he was with Central Research Laboratory and Mechanical Engineering Research Laboratory of Hitachi Ltd. During this time, he was involved in the research on modeling and control for mechanical systems and visual guidance of mobile robots.

Since 1994, he is with the Faculty of Engineering of Osaka Institute of Technology. His current interests are stochastic and computational aspects in cooperative information systems.

PARALLEL TOOLS FOR COLORED IMAGE PROCESSING*

VINCENT LOZANO

Site GIAT Industries 3, rue Javelin Pagnon
BP 505 42007 Saint-Etienne Cedex 1, France
E-mail: lozano@univ-st-etienne.fr

STÉPHANE UBÉDA and XAVIER VIGOUROUX

LIP ENS-Lyon 46, allée d'Italie
69364 Lyon Cedex 7, France
E-mail: ubeda@lip.ens-lyon.fr

Over recent years clusters of workstations have begun to replace systems of mainframes. These workstations can be used to behave as a parallel machine, and then could supply supercomputing performance at modest cost. We report an experiment of such a network within PVM framework for an industrial image analysis application.

The goal of the application is to build an automated process of textile color pattern analysis. We plan to build several tools for parallel image analysis, and among those tools, we present here first the parallelization of a quantization algorithm and a way to parallelize a color image pyramid using the Parallel Virtual Machine environment.

One important point is the use of the distributed storage that represents a set of workstations. This distribution allows the complete parallelization of the Read/Write operations.

Keywords: Distributed memory computer, parallel file access, color image processing, multiresolution techniques.

1. INTRODUCTION

Over recent years clusters of workstations have begun to replace systems of mainframes. This is essentially because of the high performance/cost ratio of these machines for most scientific/industrial applications. Another point is that workstations in industry are often idle at night and over weeks. For computational intensive problems, these "farms" can be harnessed to behave as a parallel machine, and this can be a way to obtain supercomputing performance at moderate cost. Finally, the code developed to run on a cluster of workstations can also be executed on a massively parallel machine only making a new compilation.

We report an experiment of such a network within PVM framework for an industrial image analysis application. We are interested in a performant and flexible images analysis tools for textile pattern analysis. The goal of this application is to numerize some textile patterns made by an artist on various support, to do a segmentation and a color analysis. Object detection and extractions as well as color quantization must be made from a collection of about 1200×1200 colored picture of numerized textile pattern. At the end of the application, all information needed to manufacture the corresponding textile must be extracted from the digital picture.

*Supported by the Project Calcul Parallèle, Modélisation, Simulation, Nouvelles architectures parallèles et Développement d'applications of the Rhône Alpes Region.

Parallel Image Analysis: Tools and Models (1998) 43–62
© World Scientific Publishing Company

Partially automatic processing of such an image takes from 10 to 20 hours. The goal is to build a completely automatized version of this application doing the same processing in 1 to 2 hours. We plan to build a collection of tools for parallel images analysis. Parallel tools for color management have been already investigated for a cluster of workstations.[16] Color pyramidal decomposition of an image is another useful tool and this paper presents the initial study for the same environment: a collection of SUN workstation using the Parallel Virtual Machine environment.[6] The industrial context gives us most of the needed features of our parallel tools:

Efficient most of the human intervention must be suppressed; so some high level image analysis operation must be added to the initial application increasing the complexity of the application but the industrial partner needs drastic reduction of computing time!

Portable because the hardware on which the final application must run is not already known; it must have a good performance/price ratio in order to satisfy the industrial contraints; a network of powerful workstations seems to be a good trade-off solution; experimentation on a massively parallel computer could be interesting as well.

Flexible the application is not completely defined and several changes could be made during the conception of it; one can say that the final application will be built on the top of low-levels images processing kernel (filtering, contour detection ...) and medium-level kernels (pyramids, statistical analysis ...).

In this paper we present a parallel quantization technique and pyramidal color decomposition of the image which are standard preprocessing steps of most colored picture analysis application.

The aim of color quantization is to reduce the number of colors in an image according to a specific criterion. A usual criterion is the conservation of the aspect of the remaining picture according to visual human perception. Effectively, after such a preprocessing, the different algorithms applied to the image are all the more efficient, some noises are reduced. A lot of studies have been done to succeed in the research of a set of colors that is smaller than the original set and such that the new image is as "close" as possible to the original one.

Obviously, this is a problem of minimization of an energy function and thus the resolution of this problem is NP-complete. The classical method to solve such problems is to use an heuristic that leads to a nearly optimal solution. We present here one of these heuristics which is sequential and then transcript it to make it parallel.

Multiresolution techniques, and especially pyramids, are often used for image segmentation.[11,14] A conventional pyramid is a hierarchy of fine to coarse resolution versions of an image, where the resolution decreases usually twofold between consecutive levels. Even if there is 50 percent overlap between adjacent kernels[5] along both horizontal and vertical directions, this conventional structure is always fixed and is also too rigid to be adapted for any application. Actually, Antonisse pointed out its intrinsic limitations[1] and a more critical view of the conventional pyramidal structure evaluates its inherent problems.[4] The number of cells in the next higher level is 1/4 of that in the lower one and some applications have shown that this growth rate may be too fast. So, we use the *fractional pyramid* that has been introduced by P. J. Burt in Ref. 5 to increase the number of levels.

2. FORMALISM

2.1. Quantization

This formalism (and the sequential algorithm) is extracted from Ref. 17. Its advantage is to be simple, and nevertheless powerful. Let $\Omega = \{(r, g, b)|0 \leq r, g, b \leq 255\}$ be the *RGB color space*. We choose this color space among the different ones (see Ref. 12 for a list, or Ref. 8, p. 227) for the sake of simplicity. Furthermore, the information is distributed among each axis without predilection; the algorithms are much more simple. Let $(x, y) \in I \times I$ be the coordinates of the pixels in the original image. I is an integer set. A digital image is defined as a mapping which assigns a color to each pixel:

$$h : I \times I \rightarrow C \subset \Omega \tag{1}$$

where $C = \{c_1, c_2, \ldots, c_N\}$ is the palette and N is the total number of colors in the original image. A quantized image is defined as a mapping which assigns a new color to each pixel:

$$f : I \times I \rightarrow R \subset \Omega \tag{2}$$

You can notice that R is not necessarily a subset of C: $R = \{r_1, r_2, \ldots, r_K\}$ with $K \ll N$.

The replacement of a color c_i by a representative color $r(c_i) = (r', g', b') \in R$ will generate an error defined as:

$$||c_i - r(c_i)||^2 = (r - r')^2 + (g - g')^2 + (b - b')^2 \tag{3}$$

Now, we can compute the total error on the quantization of an image of size $||I|| \times ||I|| = M^2$ with

$$D(h, f) = \frac{1}{M^2} \sum_{(x,y)\in I\times I} ||h(x, y) - f(x, y)||^2 \tag{4}$$

If $\forall i \in \{1, \ldots, N\}, p(c_i)$ denotes the relative occurrence frequencies of the colors in the original image. The last equation may be rewritten as

$$D(h, f) = \sum_{i=1}^{N} p(c_i)||c_i - r(c_i)||^2 \tag{5}$$

Obviously, in the set of colors R, we choose the best color r_j to substitute an original color $c_i \in C$. The best color means the color that minimizes the Eq. (3). With these definitions and notations, the problem of quantization may be expressed as:

*the objective of quantization is to find a set of K colors to substitute
with the best accuracy the N colors $(N \gg K)$ of an original image.
Still according to Ref. 17, this problem is at least as difficult as the
construction of an optimal binary decision tree. This latter is known as
to be NP-Complete, thus the former problem too.*

Now, let us see the sequential algorithm that leads to a parallel algorithm.

2.2. Fractional Pyramids

Let us defined g_ℓ the level ℓ of the pyramid decomposition of an image (g_0 is the
image), $g_{\ell,i}$ the value of pixel i at level ℓ and $x_{\ell,i}$ the position of pixel i at level ℓ.
The basics concepts which defined the fractional pyramid are the followings:

- Let $r = k_1/k_2$, $k_2 < k_1 < 2k_2$, where k_1 et k_2 are positives integers.
- for every k_1 samples of g_ℓ, there will be k_2 samples of $g_{\ell+1}$,
- these samples are computed at regular intervals (r^ℓ for g_ℓ),
- the distance from $g_{\ell,i}$ to the nearest sample point of g_ℓ remains the same when i
  increases modulo k_2.

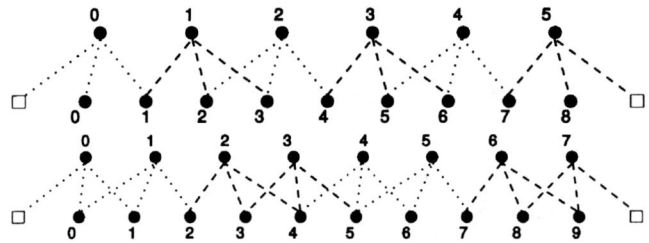

Fig. 1.   Fractional pyramid with $r = \frac{3}{2}$ and $r = \frac{5}{4}$.

Figure 1 shows an example of a fractional pyramid with two different order r
and kernels width set to 1.

We have generalized the construction of such a pyramid. For an order equal to
k_1/k_2, the three last conditions implies that there will be k_2 generating kernels.

Let w_θ be the kernel which generates the nth element of g_ℓ, then θ is defined by:

$$\theta = k_2 - 1 - n \mod k_2$$

The following formulas give the way to generate the sample $g_{n,\ell}$ with kernels of
width m, in function of θ:

- $\theta \geq \lfloor \frac{k_2}{2} \rfloor$

$$g_{n,\ell} = \begin{cases} \displaystyle\sum_{i=-m}^{m-1} w_{i+m} g_{\lfloor nr+i \rfloor, \ell-1} & k_1 + k_2 \text{ even} , \\[2em] \displaystyle\sum_{i=-m}^{m} w_{i+m} g_{\lfloor nr+i \rfloor, \ell-1} & k_1 + k_2 \text{ odd} . \end{cases} \tag{6}$$

- k_2 is odd and $\theta = \frac{k_2-1}{2}$

$$g_{n,\ell} = \begin{cases} \displaystyle\sum_{i=-m}^{m} w_{i+m} g_{\lceil nr+i \rceil, \ell-1} & k_1 + k_2 \text{ even}, \\[2em] \displaystyle\sum_{i=-m}^{m-1} w_{i+m} g_{\lceil nr+i \rceil, \ell-1} & k_1 + k_2 \text{ odd}. \end{cases} \tag{7}$$

- $\theta < \lfloor \frac{k_2}{2} \rfloor$

$$g_{n,\ell} = \begin{cases} \displaystyle\sum_{i=-m}^{m-1} w_{i+m} g_{\lceil nr+i \rceil, \ell-1} & k_1 + k_2 \text{ even}, \\[2em] \displaystyle\sum_{i=-m}^{m} w_{i+m} g_{\lceil nr+i \rceil, \ell-1} & k_1 + k_2 \text{ odd}. \end{cases} \tag{8}$$

Most object delineation algorithms use a down-top process to detect spots[13] in the upper levels. To characterize a spot, it is a good method to compare the absolute and relative contrast of a pixel with its sons and father. Such spots then define roots for a top-down process which reconstruct the objects that have been delineated.

In order to define the "natural" father N of a sample n at level ℓ, we compute the closest sample N at level $\ell+1$ to sample n at level ℓ. Thus N is given by:

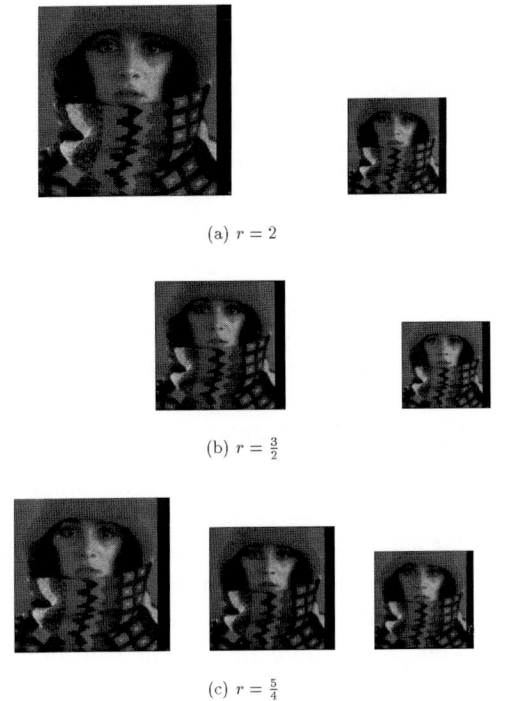

(a) $r = 2$

(b) $r = \frac{3}{2}$

(c) $r = \frac{5}{4}$

Fig. 2. Example of fractional pyramids of color image.

$$N = E\left(\frac{n - \frac{1}{2}(r - 1)}{r}\right) \tag{9}$$

Figure 2 shows two examples of construction of a fractional pyramid. The first line (Fig. 2(a)) consist of two levels of the "conventional" gaussian pyramid, while the next two lines (Figs. 2(b) and 2(c)) concerns two fractional pyramid with a reduction of $\frac{3}{2}$ and $\frac{5}{4}$.

We are now working on a color image segmentation process based on the pyramid tool. By increasing the number of levels in the structure let us think that the segmentation process will be more relevant. The textile origin of our images, involves that we deal with both fine and coarse patterns, now the fractional pyramid is a flexible tool to detect such a pattern.

In our implementation of the fractional pyramidal we add a color quantization process. The aim of color quantization is to reduce the number of colors in an image according to a specific criterion. A usual criterion is the conservation of the aspect of the remaining picture according to visual human perception. Effectively, after such a preprocessing, the different algorithms applied to the image are all the more efficient and some noises are reduced. A lot of studies have been done to succeed in the research of a set of colors that is smaller than the original set and such that the new image is as "close" as possible to the original one.

Obviously, this is a problem of minimization of an energy function and thus the resolution of this problem is NP-complete. The classical method to solve such problems is to use an heuristic that leads to a nearly optimal solution.

Color image analysis is still limited because of a very important amount of data. To reduce this information without a loss of relevant data, the pyramidal approach is well adapted.[9,10] Indeed, it enables a spatiocolor approach considering color and spatial distribution at the same time. Considering the three dimensional color space, one pyramid is defined for each component and the color pyramid is then obtained by combining the three pyramids. Some applications have confirmed that color information is well propagated through the pyramid and in accordance with human visual analysis.

We then work at present on the way to use the concept of fractional local pyramids in color image analysis. At present time, the simplest quantization technique has been coupled with a fractional pyramid generation, and the computing of both is distributed onto a LAN of SUN workstation.

2.3. Parallel Processing

A Local Area Network of workstations is not at all a parallel machine. This is a set of processors, but the communication network is a bus. First, it implies that there is only one communication at a time; second, there is no topology. The model is thus clear, the global communication time is the sum of all the communication times.

Usually, we consider the cost (in time units) of communications as a $\beta + l.\tau$ function. l is the length of the message (in information units), τ is the "bandwidth" (i.e. the number of information units per time units) and β is the startup time due to the buffer allocation. Here, this model is enhanced by another term in the sum because the startup time is not a constant but also depends on the length of the message. Indeed, the buffer allocations seem to be implemented as a linked list of small buffera, thus the buffer construction is built up from several parts. This implies that the communication costs are now $\beta_1 + \lfloor l/\text{size(small buffer)} \rfloor \beta_2 + L\tau$.

2.3.1. PVM

We decide to use PVM with Sun WorkStations. PVM (stands for "Parallel Virtual Machine")[2,3,7] is a widely used package with two main properties: portability and heterogeneity. It can be installed and used by anybody without any privileges. It can be used on one workstation as well as on a set of parallel machines. All these points make PVM as attractable for a newcomer in parallel processing, as for an expert: they can use their usual programming environment to test their program before execute them on one of the architectures they are used to.

As we have already written, the problem of PVM on a LAN (Local Area Network) of workstations[a] resides in the network itself. First, the network is a shared bus, thus only one communication takes place at a time on the entire network. The second problem is that there is no topology. Thus no optimization may be done to make the communication faster. These remarks lead us not to optimize the communication phase, because it would be a lack of time. The communication layout is therefore very simple. This point is very important for the design of the algorithm, because we must minimize the communications in the system, not to make them sequential.

Figure 3 shows the internal behavior of PVM by displaying evidently the buffer allocation. Each buffer size is 32768 bits (i.e. 4096 bytes).

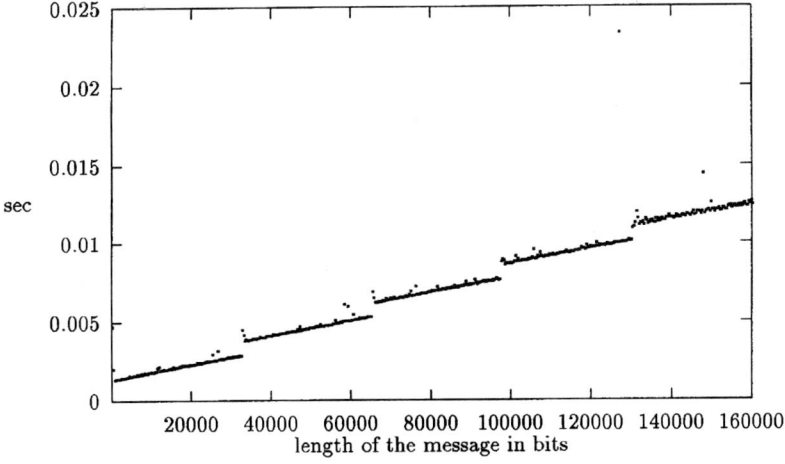

Fig. 3. Communication time with PVM 3.3.7 (option DataDefault).

---

[a]and even more for a WAN (Wide Area Network)

$$\text{time} = \beta_1 + \lfloor l/32768 \rfloor \beta_2 + L\tau \qquad (10)$$

where

$$\beta_1 \approx 1200 \ \mu\sec$$

$$\beta_2 \approx 1000 \ \mu\sec$$

$$\tau \approx 0.04882 \ \mu\sec.b^{-1} \Rightarrow 20 \ \text{Mbit.s}^{-1}$$

Be careful that τ, is not the band width because the time to send 20 Mbit according to Eq. (10) is not 1 second but a lot more: 1.6 seconds.

If we want to use a simple evaluation of the communication time, we can try to find the line crossing the middle of each segment. The equation of such a line is $y = 0.074x + 812$ where x unit is bits and y μsec. The band width is then more realistic with 13.5 Mbits.s^{-1}. This value is nevertheless too large.

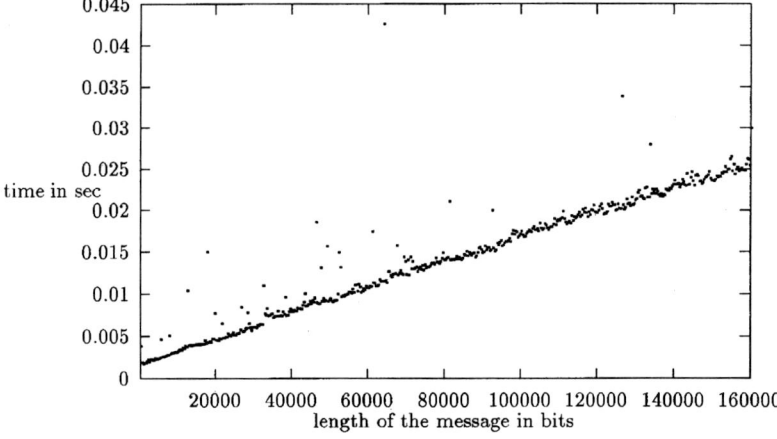

Fig. 4. Communication time with PVM 3.3.7 (option DataDefault) with network load.

Figure 4 is the same test with the same conditions but at different moments (few seconds after Fig. 3). It shows how the behavior of PVM may change with the network occupation. The band width is 6.5 Mbits.s^{-1} and the startup 1500 μsec.

The communication time of Fig. 5 shows the behavior of PVM when the programmer uses the `DataInPlace` strategy. First, this strategy avoids to copy the buffer to send; and second, it does not use the XDR library to encode the data. This strategy is worse than the first one as long as the size of the message is greater than 1024 integers (i.e. 4096 bytes). The formula expressing the communication time is then

$$\text{time} = \beta_1 + \lfloor l/65536 \rfloor \beta_2 + L\tau \qquad (11)$$

where

$$\beta_1 \approx 3000 \ \mu\sec$$

$$\beta_2 \approx 100 \ \mu\sec$$

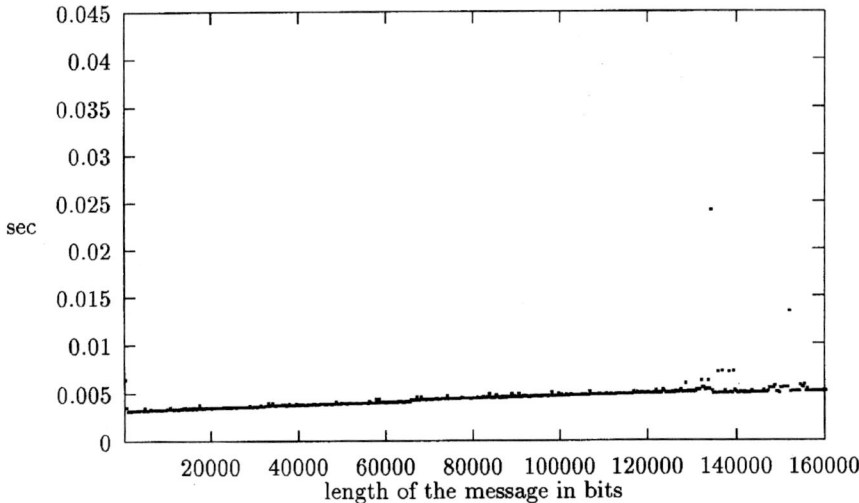

Fig. 5. Communication time with PVM 3.3.7 (option DataInPlace).

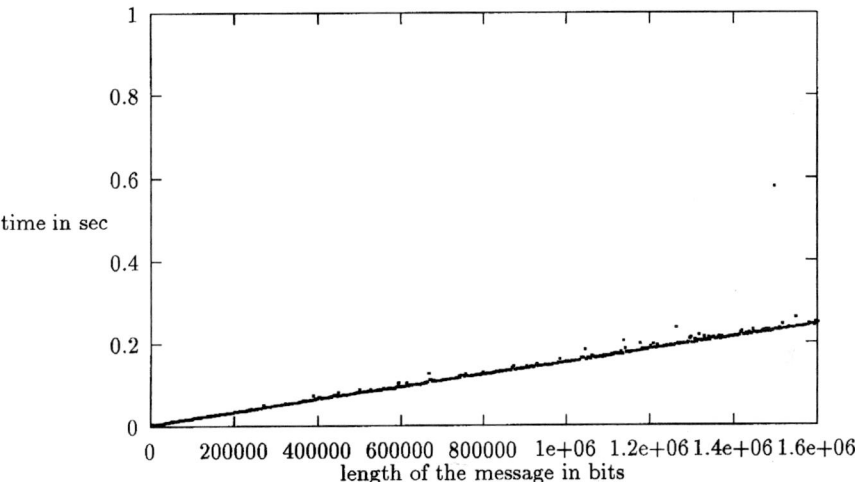

Fig. 6. Communication time with PVM 3.3.7 on very large messages.

$$\tau \approx 14 \ \mu \sec .\text{bit}^{-1} \Rightarrow 71 \ \text{Mbit.s}^{-1},$$

this band width is larger than the theoretical maximum internet band width.

These values are greater than the internet theoretical band width: 10 Mbits.s^{-1}. In fact, the size of the messages makes this result not significant (they are too short). When we choose a larger scale, we can see that the band width is not larger than the theoretical but rather 6.5 Mbit.s^{-1} (see Fig. 6) in the standard case and 8 Mbit.s^{-1} (see Fig. 7) with the option DataInPlace.

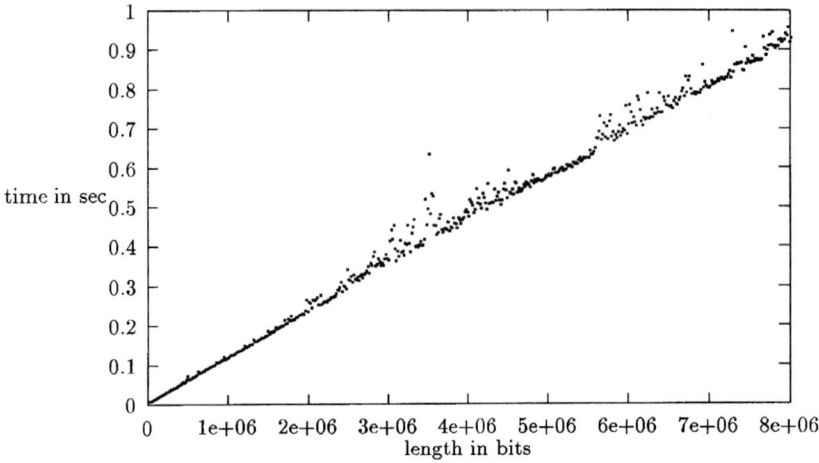

Fig. 7. Communication time with PVM 3.3.7 (option DataInPlace) on very large messages.

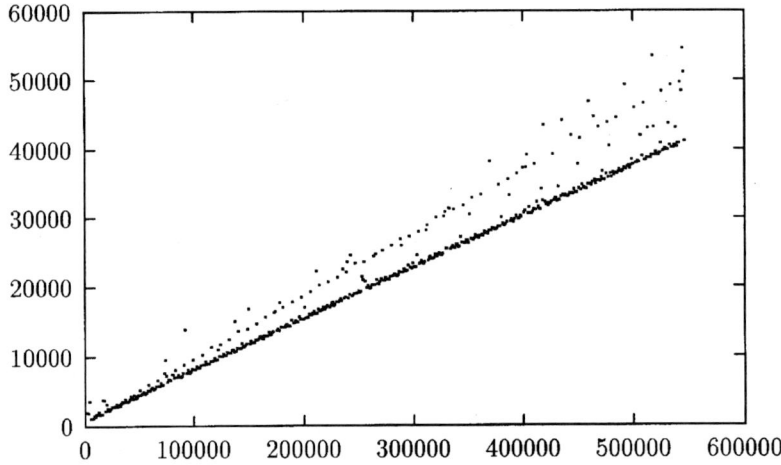

Fig. 8. Read operation on remote host (μsec as a function of file length).

2.3.2. Parallel I/O

As we have already said in the previous section, the workstations offer different sites to put data. Thanks to this, we distribute the image on different hard disks. We choose to divide the image horizontally because of the fact that a scene is usually divided this way. For instance, the sky is at the top, the ground at the bottom, ... Then, the number of different colors on each machine will be reduced.

At the end of the treatment, the image slice is also stored on a local disk. A merging phase is then added to the execution to create the global quantized image. We test the speed of the Read/Write operations to see the behavior of the remote disk operation. Figure 8 shows the result of this test.

3. PARALLEL TOOL

This section presents the parallelization of the color quantization technique, with experimental results and implementation details. It also presents the current stage of the integration of fractional pyramid technique in the tool. At the moment, this process is not complete but standard parallel pyramid decomposition runs.

3.1. Parallel Quantization

3.1.1. Sequential quantization algorithm

The idea of this algorithm[17] is to construct, for the original image, the 3D histogram of the occurrence frequency of each color. In other terms, we construct a (discrete) RGB-cube that has in the elementary point (r_0, g_0, b_0) the number of pixels with this color. Once this cube is constructed, the algorithm consists in creating a set of boxes (englobing a set of elementary colors) that will be associated with one and only one color: **the representative color**. Different solutions exist to get a color from a box $(r_1, g_1, b_1) - (r_2, g_2, b_2)$:

- we have to choose the color that will represent the box.
  - the mean of the colors $(\frac{r2-r1}{2}, \frac{g2-g1}{2}, \frac{b2-b1}{2})$,
  - the median, ...
- then we have to choose the part of the RGB-space that will be reduced to this color
  - the box itself,
  - the elements of the 3D Voronoi partition of the space, ...

The solutions are numerous. We test different solutions and the result is always (perceptibly) similar. After having seen the way to correspond an original color to a representative color, Table 1 shows how to construct these boxes.

Table 1. Sequential algorithm.

1. initialization of one unique sub-box containing the entire cube
2. For the number of wanted Colors do
2.1. Select the sub-box with the largest variance (*the one which division will separate the larger number of points in the RGB-Space*),
2.2. For Each Dimension do
2.2.1. Project the distribution according to dimension,
2.2.2. Select the optimal threshold that will create the most different two sub-boxes (*with the most different representative color*),
2.2.3. Compute the weighted sum of the variance of the two intervals
2.3. The division plane is the one that is perpendicular to the axis with the minimum weighted sum of projected variances and passes through the optimal threshold.
2.4. Divide the box into two sub-boxes.

More roughly, the algorithm presented in Table 1 consists in starting with one box and dividing it correctly until we have obtained the right number of sub-boxes.

Each sub-box is then représentative of one colour. At each step, the algorithm chooses the best box to divide. This box is the one in which the division will create the two most separate classes (I mean, two colors as distinct as possible).

This algorithm is very easy to implement on a sequential computer. But, on a parallel computer, the amount of data to exchange is prohibitive. Thus, the parallel version is slightly different than the sequential one; generally, it has been simplified.

3.1.2. Resulting choices and algorithm

The central idea of the distributed algorithm is the same as the sequential one, but two things must be distributed: data and computation.

- concerning the data, the image is distributed on different processors, and even on different hard disks. Effectively, using PVM on workstations makes it possible to use their disks. This way, the load phase, which is very costly for image processing problems, becomes lighter. The distribution is made along horizontal blocks.
- the computation is also distributed: each processor computes one part of the box division.

Three structures are very important in this algorithm: the RGB-Cube, the box and, obviously, the image.

The **RGB-Cube** This cube is a 3D array of integers. Each cell contains the number of pixels with this color. The problem of this cube is that it may be very sparse.

The first optimization consists in reducing the number of bits assigned to each colors: for instance, if each color is coded on 8 bits in the original image, we can choose a cube with only 5 bits. Then each cell is no more 1 color but $(2^{8-5})^3 = 512$.

The second optimization we choose to reduce the amount of empty cells, is to make local bounds.

- The red dimension is limited by a $R_{\min}$ and $R_{\max}$,
- Each plan $r \in [R_{\min}, R_{\max}]$ as green local bounds $G_{\min}(r)$ and $G_{\max}(r)$,
- Finally each line $r \in [R_{\min}, R_{\max}]$ and $g \in [G_{\min}(r), G_{\max}(r)]$ has blue local bounds $B_{\min}(r, g)$ and $B_{\max}(r, g)$.

The domain of computation is then greatly reduced. A test with a 5 bits RGB-cube has shown a gain of 85%!!! The order in which we consider the color must not have any consequence in the compression rate because the information is equally distributed amongst the three axes. This way, in mean, the results must be the same with six different axes enumeration: RGB, RBG, GBR, GRB, BRG, BGR. Besides, the compression rate is not the best we should obtain because of this RGB space.

Lastly, the third optimization, is to consider a cell with the value 1 as a void cell. This optimization increases the performance of the second one. But, this optimization should reduce the quality of the produced image; in fact, the result is not (perceptibly) different.

The **Box**. Once the cube of frequencies is constructed, a box only consists of three intervals: one for red, one for green and one for blue. The frequencies are shared with the cube; thus, the information is not repeated. Other fields are added to make it possible to compute the necessary information for the segmentation algorithm. Typically, we have the projection along each direction (sum, weight, array of projected values) and the mean.

The **Image**. The source image is a raster file with 8 bits per color, the resulting image is also written in such a format.

3.1.3. Communication with the RGB-cube

As we have seen in the previous section, the cube is optimized not to send large messages and thus to reduce the communication cost. In practice, we exchanged only the interesting data (i.e. a subset of each color interval). This optimization has shown its efficiency by greatly reducing the communication cost. As we have to merge the cube, we could think that a merging binary tree would have been the best solution. With PVM on a set of workstations, this is a worse solution than merging everything on a single processor.

First, the number of communications is larger in the tree. We have seen the communications are sequential on a set of workstations, thus the number of communications corresponds to the time spent by the global system. Let us count the number of communications in both cases.

- The case of the tree: if p represents the number of processors, then, whatever the shape of the merging tree, the number of internal nodes is equal to $p - 1$. As each internal node needs two communications (for both entries), the number of communications is equal to $2(p - 1)$,
- The case of the local merging: the number of communications is obviously $p - 1$.

Furthermore, the message lengths in the first case is larger than in the second, because, as we merge the data, the cube becomes larger and larger. Intuitively, the better is the linear merge.

3.1.4. Parallel quantization algorithm

Table 2. Parallel algorithm.

1. Distribute the source image if necessary.
2. Distribute the parameters (size of the cube, number of wanted colors).
3. For each Processor Do
   - 3.1. compute the RGB-cube
   - 3.2. send it to the master who merges it
   - 3.3. receive the complete one
   - 3.4. compute a part of the colors (i.e. some boxes)
   - 3.5. send them to the master who merges them
   - 3.6. receive the complete set of colors
   - 3.7. compute the new palette
   - 3.8. apply it to the part of the image.
4. Merge the global quantized image.

For the sake of communication reduction, we do not want to have more exchanges than two broadcasts (one for image, one for cube). This implies during the color computation that no processor exchanges data. Thus, every one must have a coordinated behavior. This is done by numbering each processor. Each processor only knows how many processors are in the machine and the number of wanted colors.

Let us choose one processor among the $p = 2^n$. Its number i written in binary is $i_0 i_1 \ldots i_{n-1}$. This number is the code of the tree branch to compute: each box is divided into two sub-boxes. The lowest is the number 0 and the highest the number 1. Obviously, several processors compute the same part, but at the end, they conclude by a unique calculus (Fig. 9).

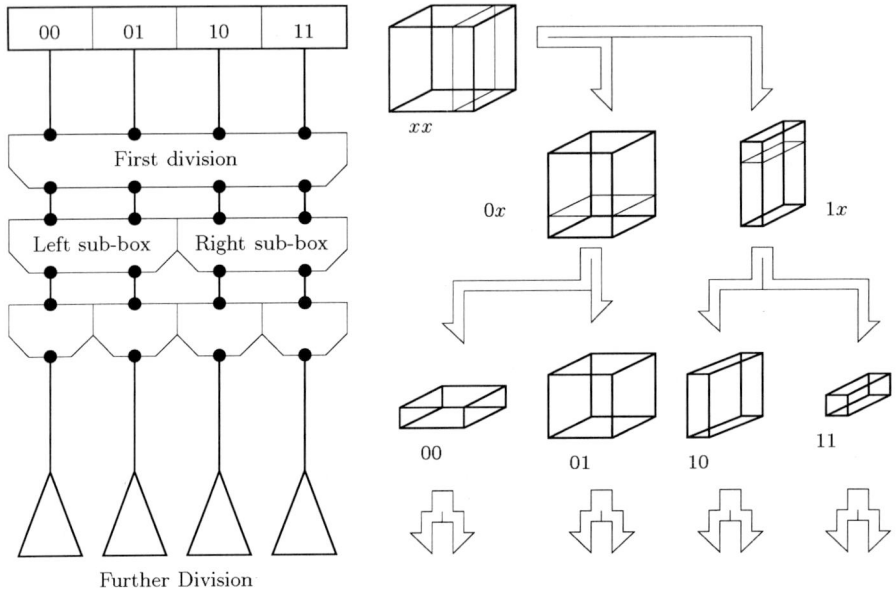

Fig. 9. Example of Work repartition with 4 processors.

The problem of this method comes from the fact that some boxes may become void. Then, it is impossible to divide them. Thus, the number of colors a processor obtains is less than the expected number. Furthermore, it is very difficult to avoid this problem without exchanging a lot of data (all to all). In fact, this problem is not very important because if a box cannot be divided, it implies that no division is really needed, so such a division would have been with no effect on the resulting image.

3.1.5. Performances

First, the different optimizations on the structures lead to very good performances (even in sequential). For instance, on a single processor, the time to execute the program on a 600×303 image with a 6 bits cube and a 64 colors palette is 5 sec on a Sparc5!!!

But, as the computation is very sharp, the communication cost is very important in the total time, thus, with 2 hosts the total time is 4.5 sec.

Table 3. Different execution times.

Number of hosts	time (sec)			
	5 bits		6 bits	
	64 cols	128 cols		64 cols
1	1.6	2	5.5	5
2	1.4	1.8	4.9	4.5
4	1.6	2	8.8	4.7

3.2. Pyramid Decomposition

Parallelization of a pyramidal algorithm must solve the problem of data distribution onto a LAN of workstations and the parallelization of the process. The aim of parallelization is to obtain an application that runs faster and/or to be able to solve problems that do not fit into the memory of a sequential machine. These two goals may be contradictory. The efficiency of a parallel algorithm is defined as the sequential execution time divided by the product of the parallel execution time with the number of processors. The execution time on a parallel machine is made of computation time and communication overhead. To obtain a good efficiency the processing time must be evenly distributed onto the different processors and the communication overhead must be as small as possible.

For the pyramidal construction process, one can see that an equidistribution of the data structure also solves the distribution processing time. In order to achieve a perfect data distribution as well as perfect load balancing, we must equidistribute each level of the pyramid onto the processors. There exists two ways to distribute an $N \times N$ image onto P processors. We can divide the image in $\sqrt{P} \times \sqrt{P}$ blocks of size $N/\sqrt{P} \times N/\sqrt{P}$ or in P blocks of size $N \times N/P$. The first solution minimizes the amount of neighboring data between blocks and the second solution minimizes the number of messages exchanged for non local data access.

As we already said, the time to exchange a message of size l can be modeled as a startup time, β and a transfer time, $l \times \tau$. On a LAN of workstations, the startup time is very high. We must minimize the number of communication phases in the parallelization (i.e. the number of messages to be exchanged). We chose the second data distribution strategy: the image is divided onto the processor in P blocs of N/P consecutive lines to reduce the number of startup which strongly decrease the efficiency.

Building the pyramid needs a communication for each level of the pyramid in order to access non local data. This is almost prohibitive. We want to reduce the number of communication phases. Let us think first of a standard image to image filtering process. We compute the value of a pixel in iteration i using the previous value of this pixel and the value of its neighbor at iteration $i - 1$. If we compute the image at each iteration without any communication, we only get partial results at each iteration (see Fig. 10). The missing data can be built using a single communication step. This communication is an exchange of the border of the "prism" built during the first step. This "prism" is nothing more than the border of the area we succeed to compute with local data. With this information, each processor can compute the value for the missing pixels at each level.

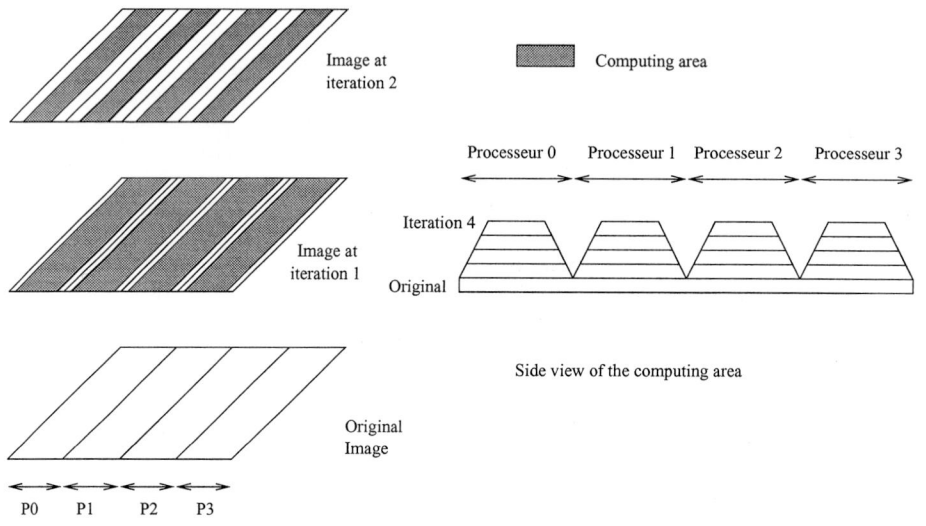

Fig. 10.   Iterative neighboring image to image parallel operation.

In the pyramidal construction process, the image built at each iteration is reduced by constant factor. And thus, the number of rows needed at each iteration to compute the missing data will increase at each iteration. This solution cannot be very efficient. The final solution is to distribute the data with a overlap area. This overlap area must be big enough to allow the construction of some levels of the pyramid without any communication. After some levels of the pyramid have been built, the overlap area is be updated. But the amount of data is reduced. This solution increases the number of communication steps but reduces the amount of exchanged data. The side effect is that the amount of memory needed on each processor is bigger than the image block allocated on this processor. This induces a reduction of the size of the biggest image which can be computed. If we want to build several levels of the pyramid this overlap area can be very important and correspond to, more or less, the complete image. Note that this solution is also easy to implement and to link with other existing parallel image processing applications.

At the current stage, the standard pyramidal construction (with a reduction of a factor 2) is running. There still exist some problems to solve with the parallel fractional algorithm. There exists a tradeoff between the overlapping area that reduces the maximal problem size and the efficiency of the algorithm. This parallel pyramidal tool will be linked using a parallel color quantization tool already developed with the same method.[16]

4. CONCLUSION AND FUTURE WORK

The paper reports the current stage of a parallel pyramidal tool for color images. This is a part of a project involved by the *Région Rhône-Alpes* and link with an industrial application in the field of textile analysis. The goal of the application is to build an automated process of textile color pattern analysis.

Our target architecture is a LAN of workstation which has a high performance/cost ratio for most scientific/industrial applications. Another point is that workstations in industry are often idle at night and over weeks. For computational intensive problems, these "farms" can be harnessed to behave as a parallel machine, and this can be a way to obtain supercomputing performance at moderate cost.

At the current stage, the standard pyramidal construction is running. There are some little problems to solve with the parallel fractional algorithm. We must also balance the problem of memory induced by overlapping area and the efficiency of the algorithm. This parallel pyramidal tool will be linked soon with the parallel color quantization tool already developed.[16]

The experimental results of the quantization algorithm have shown how communications are costly with PVM on a LAN of workstations. However, the segmentation algorithm described in this paper must have a very good behavior on a multi-processor machine. But, we have not yet tried to translate it. Future work concerns the improvement of the error criteria.

The error we have chosen, in the RGB space, does not have perceptive reality but this is the most intuitive. Nevertheless Ref. 15 explains that this error is insufficient because it does not take into account the spatial correlation between two adjacent pixels. We could define an error which is not a simple pixel to pixel comparison. For instance, if we take into account the difference between two adjacent pixel colors we would be closer to the perception. Such an error may be defined by applying a 3×3 convolution mask on each pixel in both images and then making the difference between these two results. The mask may be as for the edge detection:

$$u_0 = \begin{bmatrix} 0 & -1 & 0 \\ -1 & 4 & -1 \\ 0 & -1 & 0 \end{bmatrix} \qquad u_1 = \begin{bmatrix} -1 & -1 & -1 \\ -1 & 8 & -1 \\ -1 & -1 & -1 \end{bmatrix} \qquad u_2 = \begin{bmatrix} 1 & -2 & 1 \\ -2 & 4 & -2 \\ 1 & -2 & 1 \end{bmatrix}$$

As the sum of the weights of these filters is 0, these filters make each pixel totally relative to its environment. In this method, one image a little bit more red than another will be very close to this last one.

The second optimization consisting of considering only the interval of value with non empty cells is inherently not the best one in the RGB space because of the cube itself. Effectively, a scene is composed of different objects. Each object will have its own color with different brightness due to the light reflexion angles. Thus, in the RGB space, each object will create a segment of colors representing the color of the object with different brightness. This segment, as we can see in Fig. 11 does not follow one dimension but is rather parallel to the line $r = g = b$: $r = g + \alpha_g = b + \alpha_b$ (this is a simplistic formalization). And such a segment makes the optimization less efficient. If we had chosen another space like Hue-Saturation-Brightness or Hue-Lightness-Saturation the result would have been much better.

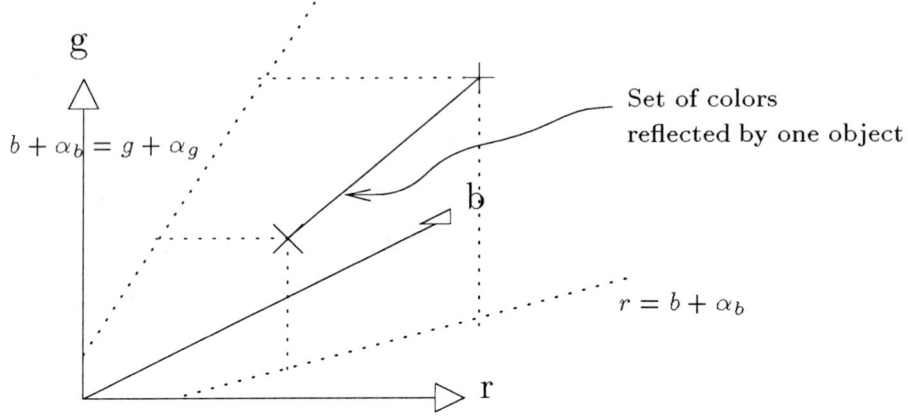

Fig. 11.　Set of colors reflected by one object.

REFERENCES

1. H. J. Antonisse, "Image segmentation in pyramids", *Comput. Graphics Image Process.* **19** (1982) 367–383.
2. A. Beguelin, J. Dongarra, A. Geist, R. Manchek, K. Moore and V. Sunderman, "PVM and HeNCE: tools for heterogeneous network computing", in *Environments and Tools for Parallel Scientific Computing*, vol. 6 of *Advances in Parallel Computing*, eds. J. Dongarra and B. Tourancheau, Saint Hilaire du Touvet, France, September 1992. CNRS-NSF, Elsevier Science Publishers – North Holland, pp. 139–154.
3. A. Beguelin, J. Dongarra, A. Geist, R. Manchek and V. Sunderam, "A users' guide to PVM (parallel virtual machine)", Rapport Technique ORNL/TM-11826, Oak Ridge National Laboratory, University of Tennessee, July 1991.
4. M. Bister, J. Cornelis and A. Rosenfeld, "A critical view of pyramid segmentation algorithms", *Patt. Recogn. Lett.* **11** (1990) 605–617.
5. P. J. Burt, "Fast filter transforms for image processing", *Comput. Graphics Image Process.* **16** (1981) 20–51.
6. J. J. Dongarra, A. Geist, R. Manchek and W. Jiang, "Using PVM 3.0 to run grand challenge applications on a heterogenous network of parallel computers", in *Sixth SIAM Conf. Parallel Processing for Scientific Computing*, eds. R. F. Sincovec, D. E. Keyes, M. R. Leuze, L. R. Petzold and D. A. Reed, SIAM, 1993, pp. 873–877.
7. G. Geist and V. Sunderman, "Experiences with network based concurrent computing on the PVM system", Rapport Technique ORNL/TM-11760, Oak Ridge National Laboratory, January 1991.

8. R. Gonzalez and R. Woods, *Digital Image Processing*, Addison-Wesley Publishing Company, 1993.
9. M. D. Levine, "Region analysis using pyramid data structure", *Comput. Vision Models*, eds. S. Tanimoto and A. Klinger, New York, 1980, pp. 57–100.
10. J. Liu and Y. H. Yang, "Multiresolution color image segmentation", *IEEE Trans. Patt. Anal. Mach. Intell.* **16**, 7 (1994) 689–700.
11. V. Lozano, H. Konik and B. Laget, "Objects delineation via local fractional pyramids", *IEEE Image and Multidimensional and Digital Signal Processing Workshop* (Belize), 1996.
12. C. Poyton, "Frequently asked questions about colour", Fetched at Charles@mail. north.net, Toronto, CAN, 1994.
13. A. Rosenfeld and A. C. Sher, "Detection and delineation of compact objects using intensity pyramids", *Patt. Recogn.* **21**, 2 (1988) 147–151.
14. S. Tanimoto and T. Pavlidis, "A hierarchical data structure for picture processing", *Comput. Graphics Image Process.* **4** (1975) 104–119.
15. A. Tremeau, M. Calonnier and B. Laget, "Color quantization error in terms of perceived image quality", in *IEEE Proc. Acoustics, Speech and Signal Process.*, Adelaide, Australia, 1994.
16. S. Ubéda and X. Vigouroux, "Parallel image quantization using lan of workstations", in *IWPIA'4 Conference*, Lyon, France, 1995.
17. S. J. Wan, P. Prusinkiewicz and S. K. M. Wong, "Variance-based color image quantization for frame buffer display", *Color Res. Appl.* **15**, 1 (1990).

Vincent Lozano is a doctoral student at the Institut de l'Ingénierie de la Vision at the Université Jean Monnet at Saint-Etienne, France. He received a degree in engineering from the École Nationale d'Ingénieurs de Saint-Etienne in 1993. He is now finishing his doctoral thesis on image processing.

His main interests concern color image processing and multiresolution techniques.

Stéphane Ubéda received the Ph.D. degree in computer science from the Ecole Normale Supérieure de Lyon in 1992 where he was a member of the Laboratoire de l'Informatique du Parallélisme during 1990–93 (The High Performance Computing Lab). During 1992–93, he was assistant professor in the Swiss Federal Institute of Technology, Lausanne, in the Theoretical Computer Science Laboratory (LITH). He is currently assistant professor in the Université Jean Monnet, Saint-Etienne, France.

His scientific interests are parallel algorithms and complexity for image processing, computational geometry and combinatorial optimization.

Xavier-Francois Vigouroux graduated in 1996 from the Ecole Normale Supérieure of Lyon with a Ph.D. in computer science. He has studied distributed computing and monitoring information gathered from very large systems.

During his Ph.D. he also worked on image processing on parallel machines or LAN. He is now working as an R&D engineer on fault tolerant systems and high availability for HP-Grenoble in Telecom Network Division.

Photograph of X. Vigouroux is unavailable.

ASYNCHRONOUS RELAXATION OF MORPHOLOGICAL OPERATORS: A JOINT ALGORITHM-ARCHITECTURE PERSPECTIVE

F. ROBIN, G. PRIVAT and M. RENAUDIN*

France Telecom/CNET-Grenoble
BP 98, 38243 Meylan Cedex, France
E-mail: gilles.privat@cnet.francetelecom.fr

Asynchronous dynamics are introduced for the iterative computation of morphological image filters. We propose a fine-grain asynchronous algorithmic- architectural model that exploits these new possibilities to improve the convergence efficiency of such operators over standard sequential-recursive or parallel-synchronous update modes. We conclude with VLSI design perspectives and show how asynchronism can be exploited both at functional and architectural levels.

Keywords: Asynchronous iterations, mathematical morphology, image processing, asynchronous VLSI circuits, parallel architectures.

1. INTRODUCTION: MORPHOLOGICAL FILTERS FOR IMAGE SEGMENTATION

The morphological approach to unsupervised image segmentation is very attractive because it is simple, robust, and well-adapted to many different types of images. We start as an example from the algorithm presented in Ref. 11, which is based on four steps : image preprocessing, feature extraction, decision and quality estimation. The preprocessing step is a simplification phase that generates regions with constant grey-level values. It is achieved by the use of greyscale morphological filters by reconstruction, that preserve the contour information of the original image. The following focuses on these filters, the definitions of which are given below.

- The first operator of the simplification filter is an erosion or dilation of size n:
  Erosion: $y_i = \varepsilon_n(x_i) = \text{Min}\left\{x_{i+k}, k \in M_n\right\}$,
  Dilation: $y_i = \delta_n(x_i) = \text{Max}\left\{x_{i-k}, k \in M_n\right\}$,
  where the index i is the position vector of pixel x.
  Here lies the control of the simplification level. For instance, if a large structuring element M_n is used, then the segmentation result will only contain the largest components.
- The reconstruction process that "restores" the contours of the original image, while maintaining the simplification level, is based on the geodesic dilation/ erosion of size 1.
  Geodesic dilation: $y_i = \delta^{(1)}(x_i, r_i) = \text{Min}\left\{\delta_1(x_i), r_i\right\}$,

---

*Telecom Bretagne-Antenne de Grenoble

Parallel Image Analysis: Tools and Models (1998) 63–72
© World Scientific Publishing Company

Geodesic erosion: $y_i = \varepsilon^{(1)}(x_i, r_i) = \text{Max}\{\varepsilon_1(x_i), r_i\}$

These operators are applied iteratively until idempotence (convergence).

The application of iterated geodesic dilations of size 1 after an erosion of size n, the reference signal r_i being the original image, defines an opening by reconstruction. The closing by reconstruction is defined by duality, and the "open-close by reconstruction" filter, which is the actual simplification filter used for preprocessing, is the composition of an opening and a closing.

Opening by reconstruction: $y_i = \delta^{(1)}(\ldots \delta^{(1)}(\delta^{(1)}(\varepsilon_n(x_i), x_i)) \ldots, x_i)$

Closing by reconstruction: $y_i = \varepsilon^{(1)}(\ldots \varepsilon^{(1)}(\varepsilon^{(1)}(\delta_n(x_i), x_i)) \ldots, x_i)$

2. ASYNCHRONOUS RELAXATION

The canonical and straightforward parallel way to compute these iterative-convergent operators is through a globally synchronous updating mode: a full sweep of the picture is completed before the next iteration is started, all variables being updated from their previous-generation values. A recursive update mode, akin to Gauss–Seidel relaxation, is, on the other hand, known to improve convergence but is inherently sequential and directionally asymmetric. In-between, and retaining advantages from both, stand the asynchronous updating modes that have been studied for relaxation procedures,[1-3,13] partially grounded on architectural considerations. Depending on the underlying algorithm, improved convergence rates can be demonstrated, or artefacts brought up by the parallel synchronous scheme can be eliminated. In any case, supplementary degrees of freedom are made available to fine-tune some algorithmic properties.

2.1. Asynchronous Reconstruction: Elimination of Local Temporal Dependencies

The idea is to extend the parallel iteration mode to general asynchronous dynamics by relaxing local temporal constraints. From this point of view, a parallel synchronous relaxation scheme for such a convergent computation is but a particular and arbitrary way to reach the solution. The reconstruction algorithm can be moved into a set of unsynchronized local processes that can run at independent speeds. More precisely, a local calculation can be completed for each pixel, whatever the iteration numbers of the adjacent processes are. In the case of opening by reconstruction, instead of completing a global dilation of size 1 and a global pointwise "geodesic comparison" with the reference image and iterating these two steps, the algorithm can be decomposed into a set of concurrent processes (one per pixel) that iteratively calculates the "local dilation" of size 1 and apply the "geodesic" Min with the reference, without any synchronization between one another.

Asynchronous local geodesic dilation:

$$x_i^{n_i(t)+1} = \text{Min}(\text{Max}(x_{i-k}^{n_{i-k}(t+f_i(k,t))}, k \in M_1), x_i^0) \qquad (1)$$

where $n_i(t)$ is the iteration number of pixel i at time t, which explicitly shows that the iteration numbers can vary among the different pixel processes.

Figure 1 gives an example of the evolution of the iteration numbers corresponding to the different processes, in the synchronous and asynchronous cases.

Synchronous update   Asynchronous update

i	i	i
i	i	i
i	i	i

-->

i+1	i+1	i+1
i+1	i+1	i+1
i+1	i+1	i+1

i	i+1	i+1
i+1	i+1	i
i+1	i	i+1

-->

i+1	i+2	i+2
i+2	i+3	i+2
i+3	i+1	i+2

Fig. 1.

2.2. Local Processing Schemes and Convergence Speed

In Eq. (1), a further degree of freedom appears through the function $f_i(k,t)$ that specifies the time at which the neighboring state values are taken into account to compute the local Max function. This leads to the definition of two main local dynamics, corresponding to locally parallel or sequential schemes. In the parallel scheme, $f_i(k,t)$ is independent of k: each pixel process samples its neighboring state values at the same time, introducing a first level of synchronism. In the sequential scheme, asynchronism is reinforced locally, because the Max calculation takes the neighboring variables into account at different times, so that their iteration numbers may have a greater dispersion.

2.3. Computer Simulation and Convergence Result

These algorithms were simulated by selecting pixels in a random order and partially computing at each step the local operators in an internal variable, on several 8-bit 256×256 images (Fig. 2).

Image 1   Image 2   Image 3

Fig. 2. Original images and their opening by reconstruction with a diamond-shaped structuring element of size 8 (145 pixels).

The simulations showed that all the above iterative schemes reached idempotence and exactly the same solution as in the synchronous reference algorithm. The following demonstration gives a specific proof for the positive asynchronous reconstruction.

- **Definition of the synchronous and asynchronous iterative schemes:**
  Let δ be the geodesic dilation of size 1 locally defined by

$$\delta(f,r)(p) = \mathrm{Min}(r(p), \mathrm{Max}(f(p'), p' \in N(p)))\,,$$

where p is a pixel, $f(p)$ its grey level value, $r(p)$ the reference value corresponding to the same pixel in the source image, and $N(p)$ the set of pixels that belong to the 5-neighborhood of p.
Let δ_s and δ_a be respectively the synchronous and asynchronous geodesic dilations defined in a recurrent form by

$$\forall p, \delta_s^0(p) = \delta_a^0(p) = \varepsilon_n(r)(p)$$

(we start from an erosion of size n applied to the reference image) and

$$\forall j, \forall p, \delta_s^{j+1}(p) = \delta(\delta_s^j, r)(p)\,,$$
$$\forall k, \forall p, \delta_a^{k+1}(p) = \delta(\delta_a^k, r)(p) \quad \text{if } \pi(k) = p$$
$$= \delta_a^k(p) \qquad \text{if } \pi(k) \neq p\,,$$

where π is a random function that selects a pixel p at step k, such that any pixel may be selected an unbounded number of times:

$$\forall p, \forall K, \exists k > K / \pi(k) = p\,.$$

Notice that δ_s and δ_a are increasing with their iteration value:

$$\forall p, j' \geq j \Rightarrow \delta_s^{j'}(p) \geq \delta_s^j(p) \text{ and } k' \geq k \Rightarrow \delta_a^{k'}(p) \geq \delta_a^k(p)$$

and that they are bounded by the reference image:

$$\forall j, \forall p, \delta_s^j(p) \leq r(p) \text{ and } \forall k, \forall p, \delta_a^k(p) \leq r(p)\,.$$

- **Proof of the equivalence between the two schemes:**
  (i) Let us show that : $\forall j, \exists k / \forall p, \delta_a^k(p) \geq \delta_s^j(p)$.
  Clearly: $\forall p, \delta_a^1(p) \geq \delta_s^0(p)$.
  Now let's hypothesize that: $\exists j, k / \forall p, \delta_a^k(p) \geq \delta_s^j(p)$.
  Let's consider pixel p.
  Either: $\delta_a^k(p) \geq \delta_s^{j+1}(p)$,
  or: $\delta_a^k(p) < \delta_s^{j+1}(p)$.
  Let us consider the latter case.
  By definition: $\forall q, \delta_s^{j+1}(q) = \delta(\delta_s^j, r)(q) = \mathrm{Min}(r(q), \mathrm{Max}(\delta_s^j(q'), q' \in N(q)))$,

and: $\exists k' > k / \delta_a^{k'}(p) = \delta(\delta_a^{k'-1}, r)(p) = \text{Min}(r(p), \text{Max}(\delta_a^{k'-1}(p'), p' \in N(p)))$.
Then:

$$k' - 1 \geq k \Rightarrow \forall q, \delta_a^{k'-1}(q) \geq \delta_a^k(q) \geq \delta_s^j(q)$$

$$\Rightarrow \forall q, \text{Max}(\delta_a^{k'-1}(q'), q' \in N(q)) \geq \text{Max}(\delta_s^j(q'), q' \in N(q))$$

$$\Rightarrow \forall q, \text{Min}(r(p), \text{Max}(\delta_a^{k'-1}(q'), q' \in N(q))) \geq \text{Min}(r(p), \text{Max}(\delta_s^j(q'),$$

$$q' \in N(q)))$$

$$\Rightarrow \delta_a^{k'}(p) \geq \delta_s^{j+1}(p) .$$

This being true for any pixel p, let: $K = \text{Max}(k'(p))$,
then: $\forall p, \delta_a^K(p) \geq \delta_s^{j+1}(p)$.
Thus: $\exists j, k / \forall p, \delta_a^k(p) \geq \delta_s^j(p) \Rightarrow \exists k' / \forall p, \delta_a^{k'}(p) \geq \delta_s^{j+1}(p)$,
and by induction: $\forall j, \exists k / \forall p, \delta_a^k(p) \geq \delta_s^j(p)$.
(ii) Let us show that: $\forall k, \exists j / \forall p, \delta_s^j(p) \geq \delta_a^k(p)$.
Clearly: $\forall p, \delta_s^1(p) \geq \delta_a^0(p)$.
Let us hypothesize that: $\exists j, k / \forall p, \delta_s^j(p) \geq \delta_a^k(p)$.
Let us consider the pixel p such that $\pi(k+1) = p$.
Then, by definition:
$\delta_s^{j+1}(p) = \delta(\delta_s^j, r)(p) = \text{Min}(r(p), \text{Max}(\delta_s^j(p'), p' \in N(p)))$, and
$\delta_a^{k+1}(p) = \delta(\delta_a^k, r)(p) = \text{Min}(r(p), \text{Max}(\delta_a^k(p'), p' \in N(p)))$.
Thus: $\forall q, \delta_s^j(q) \geq \delta_a^k(q) \Rightarrow \delta_s^{j+1}(p) \geq \delta_a^{k+1}(p)$.

$$\text{Moreover}: \forall p' \neq p, \delta_a^{k+1}(p') = \delta_a^k(p')$$

$$\Rightarrow \forall p' \neq p, \delta_s^j(p') \geq \delta_a^{k+1}(p')$$

$$\Rightarrow \forall p' \neq p, \delta_s^{j+1}(p') \geq \delta_a^{k+1}(p') .$$

Finally: $\forall p, \delta_s^{j+1}(p) \geq \delta_a^{k+1}(p)$.
Thus: $\exists j, k / \forall p, \delta_s^j(p) \geq \delta_a^k(p) \Rightarrow \exists j' / \forall p, \delta_s^{j'}(p) \geq \delta_a^{k+1}(p)$,
and by induction: $\forall k, \exists j / \forall p, \delta_s^j(p) \geq \delta_a^k(p)$.

From (i) and (ii), and given that δ_s and δ_a are bounded, we can conclude:

$$\forall p, \text{Max}_j(\delta_s^j(p)) = \text{Max}_k(\delta_a^k(p)), \text{ i.e. } \forall p, \delta_s^\infty(p) = \delta_a^\infty(p) ,$$

which means that the synchronous and asynchronous reconstruction schemes converge to the same result.

2.4. Convergence Speed

In terms of convergence speed, an asynchronous "iteration" is defined by the random selection of the same number of pixels as in a synchronous iteration (i.e. 256×256 computations are completed, but some pixels may be selected several times while others are not considered).

Update mode	Image 1	Image 2	Image 3
Synchronous GP	194	209	250
Synchronous GS	98	140	97
Asynchronous GP-LP	105-109	114-121	128-135
Asynchronous GP-LS	142-168	161-216	159-283

Fig. 3. Numbers of iterations to reach idempotence for an opening by reconstruction (GP: Globally Parallel, GS: Globally Sequential (recursive), LP: Locally Parallel, LS: Locally Sequential).

Figure 3 compares the "convergence speed" of the different schemes that complete an opening by reconstruction, starting from the same synchronous erosion of size 8 and using a 5-pixel neighborhood.

To give orders of magnitude, the locally parallel asynchronous scheme takes nearly twice less iterations than the parallel synchronous scheme, depending on the image and the random function. The locally sequential one takes approximately 30% less to 10% more iterations, depending on the image and the order the neighboring values are taken into account, thus showing a strong directional and data dependency.

The recursive scheme sometimes converges faster than the parallel asynchronous scheme in terms of iteration count, but of course does not present any parallelism and therefore its computation time is much higher.

2.5. Local Convergence Control and Mean Activity Rate

In the previous paragraphs, all the algorithms are simulated until idempotence is reached, as a first comparison basis. However, as a convergent process is used, it may not be useful to reach this solution, because an intermediate result may be just as good for preprocessing purposes. On top of that, the system reaches an acceptable solution far before it really becomes idempotent, so that most local processes spend most of the time calculating a value that does not evolve. Keeping in mind circuit design considerations, it seems useful to add some local convergence control, that stops the evaluation of individual processes under certain conditions, and enhances the concept of processor autonomy. To stop the algorithm before idempotence, a global convergence criterion must be added. A complete solution to this point is not straightforward, but some ideas have been introduced in Ref. 6. The following local criterion has been tested, using a local counter initially set to zero:

- If the computation gives the same result as the preceding one, increase the local convergence counter unless it is already greater than one of the neighbors',
- If the result has changed, initialize the convergence counter to zero,
- If the local convergence counter and all the neighbors' counter exceed a given convergence threshold, then stop calculating and wait for one of the neighbors to start again.

Notice that if the convergence threshold is set to a large value, the convergence control does not modify the algorithm. With relatively small thresholds (like

15–20), the algorithm still converges to the same solution, but it is possible to obtain a mean activity rate smaller than 40% (the activity rate is the ratio of the pixel processes that were allowed to compute to the total number of processes). For very small thresholds (a few iterations, say 3–4), the system converges to a slightly different solution. But a very interesting result is that a mean activity rate of 10% can be reached while the difference with the reference solution stays hardly visible, even with very noisy images, and idempotence is reached even more quickly than for the asynchronous schemes without local convergence control.

2.6. Extension to Non-Convergent Operators: Asynchronous Erosions and Dilations

Given that the morphological approach proves to be very robust, the next asynchronous scheme to be examined is its extension to non-convergent operators such as erosions and dilations of size n, and the behavior of the preprocessing filter based on it. As may be expected, an asynchronous dilation (Fig. 4(b)), where each process does a local Max operation n times, leads to some fuzzy art, compared to the structured result of a synchronous dilation (Fig. 4(a)). However, the actual information contained in the asynchronous result is just as relevant as in the synchronous one. Indeed, both processing schemes lead to constant grey-level patterns of equivalent

(a) Synchronous dilation.

(b) Asynchronous dilation.

(c) Sync. open-close by recons.

(d) Async. open-close by recons.

Fig. 4.

sizes. Furthermore, the structuring element is often chosen in an arbitrary way, and the important parameter is its size, not its shape. In this sense, the asynchronous scheme is more homogeneous and general.

An interesting result is the behavior of the reconstruction process starting with this asynchronous dilation. Again, simulations prove the robustness of the approach, the difference between the synchronous (Fig. 4(c)) and the fully-asynchronous results (Fig. 4(d) shows the reconstruction based on Fig. 4(b)) being very small in regard with the preprocessing requirements, which are image simplification and homogeneous region discrimination.

For example, with the "cameraman" image, and without local convergence control, the asynchronous open-close by reconstruction reaches idempotence within $155 + 111$ iterations ($141 + 116$ with another random seed) instead of $194 + 160$ for the parallel synchronous scheme, and the final absolute (L^1) difference is less than 26000 (for an 8-bit 256×256 image).

This shows the interest of a fully asynchronous approach, retaining that the result is just as good as in the synchronous mode and that the algorithm has better properties.

3. Architectural and VLSI Design Perspectives

Mathematical morphology operators are easily decomposed into purely local operations[5] to match locally-connected parallel architectures, making high-performance implementation feasible. The operators presented above are a good application basis for the design of application-specific array processors that take advantage of such a "functional asynchronism".

We first presented some architectural and design issues related to these dynamics in Ref. 8. The ideas presented above at the functional level are applied at the architectural level, using one processing element (PE) per pixel.[10]

Such a fine-grain fully parallel asynchronous implementation takes advantage of several properties:

- each PE can be designed as a fully self-timed system, including asynchronous automata[12] and operators that generate their own completion signal,[9] so that they can calculate on a *mean-time* basis, exploiting dynamical data-dependent critical paths, contrary to synchronous systems that are designed on a worst-time basis,
- *power consumption* can be minimized because a set of unsynchronized processors move clock-transition power peaks into an averaged consumption curve, there are no clock drivers, each PE can be stopped locally, and asynchronous logic only makes necessary transitions,
- a perfectly *local* implementation is possible, with no global clock, and the use of self-timed blocks increases modularity, scalability and robustness,
- the inter-PE *communication* can be very efficient, because there is no need for synchronization during the iterated phases (but special interface circuitry must be used,[8,10] even for the local convergence control described above.

This principle can be extended to partitioned architectures that apply only an intermediate degree of parallelism, using either an LSGP (Locally Sequential Globally Parallel),[7] or a dual LPGS scheme. In the LPGS case, the array processor being of smaller size than the complete image, sweeps over the block-partitioned image, and computes a given number of asynchronous "iterations" on each block. Each block can partially overlap the previous one, to increase the "recursivity" (and thus the convergence speed) of the scheme. Contrary to the synchronous "multigeneration sweep" approach presented in Ref. 4, where incorrect bordering values propagate their effect inward and are removed from the partial result, simulations have shown that the whole block can be retained, even after more than $n/2$ iterations, where n is the block size. Trade-offs between block sizes, overlapping ratios and block iteration depths, in terms of convergence speed, I/O overhead and resulting delays have to be studied to optimize such architectures.

4. CONCLUSION

Asynchronous circuits being an already active area of research, we have attempted here to bring them up to the level of these not-so-well-known asynchronous dynamics that widen the field of algorithm design through a feedback from VLSI architecture criteria. Some morphological operators, studied in the context of new image coding techniques, prove to be good candidates for the local algorithm transformations presented here. Such a combined algorithm–architecture design opens up new opportunities to minimize power consumption and enhance locality, robustness, and efficiency through massive parallelism.

REFERENCES

1. G. Baudet, "Asynchronous iterative methods for multiprocessors", *J. ACM* **25**, 2 (1978) 226–244.
2. D. Chazan and W. Miranker, "Chaotic relaxation", *Linear Algebra and its Applications* **2** (1969) 199–222.
3. J. C. Miellou, "Algorithmes de relaxation chaotique à retards", *RAIRO*, April 1975, pp. 55–82.
4. M. Nodine, D. Lopresti and J. Vitter, "I/O overhead and parallel VLSI architectures for lattice computations", *IEEE Trans. Comput.* **40**, 7 (1991) 843–852.
5. H. Park and R. Chin, "Optimal decomposition of convex morphological structuring elements for 4-connected parallel array processors", *IEEE Trans. Patt. Anal. Mach. Intell.* **16**, 3 (1994) 304–313.
6. P. Planet and G. Privat, "Convergence control of relaxation processes with fine-grain locally-connected two-scale automata networks", *Proc. ISCAS'94*, London, June 1994.
7. G. Privat, P. Planet and M. Renaudin, "Asynchronous relaxation of locally-coupled automata networks, with application to parallel VLSI implementation of iterative image processing algorithms", *Proc. Int. Conf. Application Specific Array Processors*, October 1993.
8. G. Privat, F. Robin, M. Renaudin and B. El Hassan, "A fine-grain asynchronous VLSI cellular array processor architecture", *Proc. ISCAS'95*, Seattle, May 1995.
9. M. Renaudin and B. El Hassan, "The design of fast asynchronous adder structures and their implementation using DCVS logic", *Proc. ISCAS'94*, London, June 1994.

10. F. Robin, M. Renaudin, G. Privat and N. Van Den Bossche, "A functionally asynchronous array-processor for morphological filtering of greyscale images", *IEEE Proc. Comput. Digital Technol.*, special section on Asynchronous Architecture, **143**, 5 (1996) 273–281.
11. P. Salembier and J. Serra, "Morphological multiscale image segmentation", *Proc. SPIE Visual Communications and Image Processing* **1818** (1992) 620–631.
12. S. Unger, *Asynchronous Sequential Switching Circuits*, Wiley-Interscience, 1969.
13. A. Üresin and M. Dubois, "Sufficient conditions for the convergence of asynchronous iterations", *Parall. Comput.* **10** (1989) 83–92.

Frédéric Robin received his engineering degree in telecommunications from the Ecole Nationale Supérieure des Télécommunications de Bretagne in 1994, and is preparing a Ph.D. in electrical engineering at CNET-Grenoble, a France Telecom research center.

His thesis is focused on fine-grain concurrent and asynchronous VLSI architectures for analysis-synthesis image coding.

Gilles Privat received the engineering and doctoral degrees in signal and systems theory from ENST (Telecom Paris Institute) in 1981 and 1986, respectively. In 1982–83 he was a research associate with INPG-IMAG in Grenoble, France. Since 1983 he has been a research engineer and research group leader with CNET-Grenoble, a France Telecom research center.

His main activities have been in VLSI signal processing, parallel architecture and algorithms, automata networks and image coding. He currently works in the field of software architectures for distributed multimedia. He is a member of the editorial board of IEEE Micro. He has authored or coauthored more than 40 technical publications and 4 patents.

Marc Renaudin received his engineering degree in Signal Processing in 1987 and his Ph.D. in electrical engineering in 1990, both from the "Institut National Polytechnique" in Grenoble. In 1990 he joined the "Telecom Bretagne", a graduate school of telecommunications engineering, as assistant professor. He is now in charge of the "VLSI and Systems Design" final year option which takes place in Grenoble, France. He teaches digital signal processing, high performance computer architecture and asynchronous VLSI design.

His research activities are mainly focused on VLSI architectures for image and signal processing for telecommunication applications. He is now working on asynchronous circuits and systems design and is investigating how the asynchronous design style can be efficiently used in high speed, low power circuits.

FAST LOCAL AND GLOBAL ILLUMINATIONS
THROUGH A SIMD Z-BUFFER

C. RENAUD

Laboratoire d'Informatique du Littoral
BP 719 - 62228 Calais Cedex - France
E-mail: renaud@lil.univ-littoral.fr

The z-buffer is a well-known hidden-part removal technique commonly used by local illumination algorithms. Some global illumination approaches use this technique too, in order to approximate energy exchanges. In this paper we propose a massively parallel implementation of the z-buffer on the MP-1 machine. Efficiency is achieved by precisely studying the different stages of the algorithm, and by taking care in correctly using the SIMD control of the architecture. Local illumination models are then applied to the z-buffer algorithm, by using Gouraud and Phong's interpolations. Finally, the parallel z-buffer is used in a massively parallel radiosity algorithm. The results obtained allow to provide quickly illuminated images by decreasing dramatically the computation time required for global illumination.

Keywords: Hidden-part removal, z-buffer, local illumination, radiosity, SIMD parallelism, efficiency.

1. INTRODUCTION

The Z-buffer is a well-known hidden-part algorithm,[2] computing the foremost object at each pixel. This is performed by projecting the objects onto the screen and by computing the distance between the observer and the object for each covered pixel. Then a depth comparison in each of those pixels is performed, in order to keep the foremost object. For this purpose, a second buffer is used, so called *depth-buffer*, that stores the closest object distance, as seen from the observer through the pixel.

Eliminating the hidden parts does not provide realistic images. Realism requires to illuminate the objects, either by taking into account only direct illumination, or by using global illumination approaches.

With local illumination, an object point is supposed to be illuminated directly from point sources, or more rarely from area sources.[15] Three kinds of components are used: ambient, diffuse and specular components. Computation is only applied onto the objects' visible points. Furthermore to decrease the computation cost, interpolation techniques are applied.[12,14]

Taking into account global illumination involves more complex algorithms. Radiosity[6,11] is a powerful approach that solves this problem in case of perfectly diffuse emitters and reflectors. Visibility between objects must be determined, in order to approximate the energy exchanges between them. These visibility information are computed either by z-buffer based algorithms,[5] or by ray-casting.[26]

Local and global illumination are both time and resources expensive. Z-buffered images, locally illuminated, can be displayed in real time only by using specialized

Parallel Image Analysis: Tools and Models (1998) 73–90

hardware. Computing global illumination requires much more time and resources, as several hidden-part elimination and energy exchange stages are required.

The goal of this paper is to propose an efficient massively parallel approach for the z-buffer algorithm. Our approach provides near real-time locally illuminated images, and reduces dramatically the energy exchange stages in a radiosity algorithm. Obviously it is not our purpose to compete with hardware accelerators, but rather to provide an efficient solution for massively parallel applications that require to display images during their computation (like radiosity) without expensive data exchanges between the graphic workstation and the parallel machine.

In the next section, we present the MP-1 general architecture, and its communication facilities. Then we describe our massively parallel z-buffer, and justify our choices. The next two sections are concerned with the use of this approach for local and global illumination, each one including its own results. Finally we present some enhancements that are currently studied.

2. THE TARGET MACHINE: THE MP-1

The MP-1 machine is made up of a host workstation, a large number of processing elements (PEs), controlled by a specialized processor, so called Array Control Unit (ACU), and two communication networks. Each PE has a private memory. The main characteristic of the MP-1 is its centralized control (SIMD): each PE performs simultaneously the same instruction onto different data. Instructions and global data are broadcast by the ACU, while the local data are fetched from the PE memory. As sometimes all the PEs do not have to perform the broadcast operation, an activity flag available on each PE, allows to temporally disable the execution flow. The set of active PEs is then called the activity set. Application performances greatly depend on the size of this set.

The PEs are organized as a rectangular array of processors connected together through two communication networks: the Xnet for neighboring communications, and the Global Router for distant communications:

- The Xnet network connects each PE to its 8 nearest neighbors (see Fig. 1(a)), the PEs on the edge being connected to the PEs on the opposite edge. Each PE can then communicate with one of its neighbors but due to the SIMD feature of the MP-1 control, all the PEs must simultaneously send their messages in the same direction.
- The Global Router is able to perform connections between every pair of PEs, through a three stage hierarchy of crossbars (see Fig. 1(b)). However the PE array is implemented using 4×4 PE clusters, and only one access at a time to the Global Router is possible per cluster. Communications are then sequential inside a cluster, both for output and input (only one connection at a time is performed if several PEs, belonging to different clusters, try to make a connection to PEs handled by the same cluster).

We have implemented our approach on a 16 K PEs MP-1 (128×128 PEs array), each PE managing 64 KB RAM (1 GB global memory).

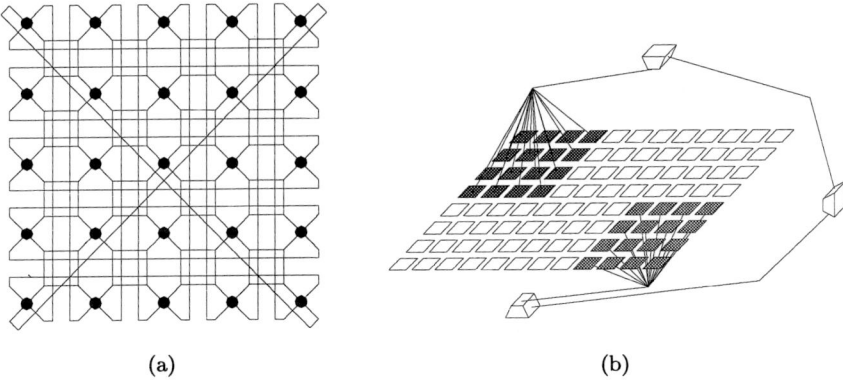

(a)   (b)

Fig. 1.   (a) Xnet. (b) Global router.

3. A MASSIVELY PARALLEL Z-BUFFER

Z-buffer is an algorithm often used when hidden-part removal occurs. But it is often used through specialized hardware available with some graphic workstations. Previous SIMD approaches for parallel z-buffer include both hardware design,[9] and software evaluation.[24] In the two cases, parallelism is achieved by using one processor per pixel, and by projecting successively all the patches. The goal of each processor is then to evaluate whether the patch covers or not its pixel. But as a large part of the processors lies outside the projection, they perform "useless" computation. Efficiency of such approach is very low, and results on general purpose computer are bad.[17]

Our goal is here to describe a SIMD parallel algorithm providing efficient use of all the PEs, and assigning them only useful work.

3.1. A SIMD Approach

We suppose first that all the objects to be z-buffered are split into convex patches. A data-parallel z-buffer involves the consideration of several patches and several pixels simultaneously. For this purpose, both the patches and the pixels are distributed across the PE array: a patch is handled by only one PE and pixels are distributed cyclicly both horizontally and vertically between the PEs (two neighboring pixels are managed by two neighboring PEs).

The sequential algorithm is made up of 5 steps: patch vertices coordinates transformation (in the point of view coordinates system); back-face culling; clipping; projection onto the screen plane and finally z-buffer. However, applying this 5-steps pipeline to several patches at the same time (one per PE) would provide low performances. Indeed, some of these 5 steps do not require the same amount of computation for different patches. For example, back-face culling can eliminate a patch, that will not be considered in the next steps. The PE managing this patch will be idle so far as the other PEs will have completed their job.

In order to achieve load-balancing, our approach proposes to cut this pipeline into three successive stages, each one being applied on all the patches before applying the next one:

- The geometric transformations are first applied on the patches. This includes coordinate transformations, back-face culling and clipping. The two first operations require the same quantity of instructions whatever the patch is. Clipping however involves small unbalancing.
- The patches are then transformed in order to be projected. This is done by computing all the lines covered by a patch. These lines are stored using a span structure.
- Finally, the spans are propagated along the pixel lines where they appear in order to really project the patches and to apply the depth-buffer algorithm.

These stages are described below, taking into account the communications involved and the load-balancing.

3.1.1. Geometric transformations

In order to achieve load-balancing, the geometric transformations are not applied successively onto an unique patch per PE. Coordinates transformation is first applied onto all the patches, in order to generate a new transformed patches list. Then back-face culling is performed and the "bad" patches are removed from the list. Finally, the patches are clipped, in order to keep only the patches that are entirely or partially into the view frustum. Applying successively the 2 first geometric transformations provides optimum balancing. Imbalance can arise during the third stage, if many patches have been removed by the back-face culling.

3.1.2. Spans computation

During this step, the patches are transformed into spans. This is performed by computing all the pixel lines covered by each projected patch. The spans are stored locally on each PE in a *span list* (see Fig. 2(a)).

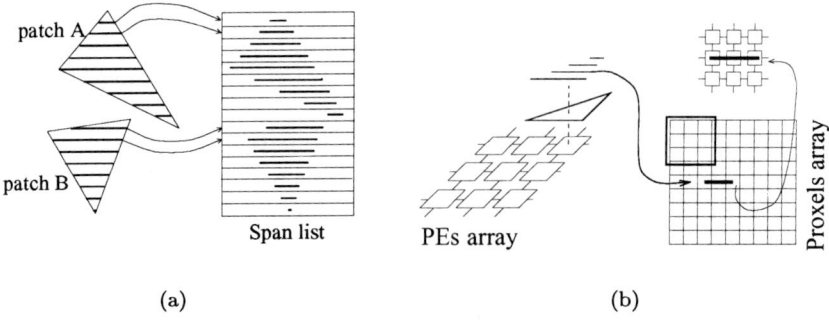

(a)   (b)

Fig. 2.   (a) Span conversion. (b) PEs association. (c) Moving the spans.

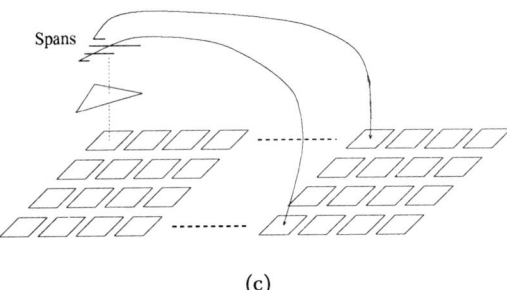

(c)

Fig. 2. (*Cont'd*).

Each list entry encloses some information about the first pixel of the span (screen coordinates, depth ...), and the span's length. We choose to compute only these information, rather than all the covered pixels, for two main reasons:

- Storing locally all the span's pixels requires too much memory. Moreover it would require a lot of communication to send them from the PE where they are generated, to the PE that manages the corresponding screen pixels.
- The number of pixels covered by the spans is very different from one patch to another. It is also a great imbalance source between the PEs.

This kind of imbalancing still occurs with the different number of spans per patch. If a PE has span-converted a patch, it has to wait for the completion of all the other PEs, the resulting span-conversion time being the time of the most consuming patch. In order to avoid loss of time, a context switching has been implemented, taking care of the SIMD control of the MP-1: when a PE detects that its current patch span conversion has been completed, it dynamically loads a new span from its span list.

Computing the spans locally to each PE requires communication in advance to perform the z-buffer step. As seen in Fig. 2(b), the pixels covered by the span are not managed by the PE that handles this span. Using the screen coordinates of the first span pixel, a PE is able to calculate the identity of the PE managing this pixel, and then to send him the span. Note that this requires only one communication per span, rather than one communication per span pixel if all the pixels have been generated by a PE. This communication is performed via the global router (Fig. 2(c)), which is better-suited for connecting any pair of PEs than the Xnet.

3.1.3. Depth-buffer

Once the previous step has been performed, each PE has a new span list, each of them beginning in a pixel managed locally. Those spans now must be depth-buffered. This step is implemented efficiently by taking advantage of the Xnet communication network and the cyclic distribution of the pixel across the PEs (see Fig. 3):

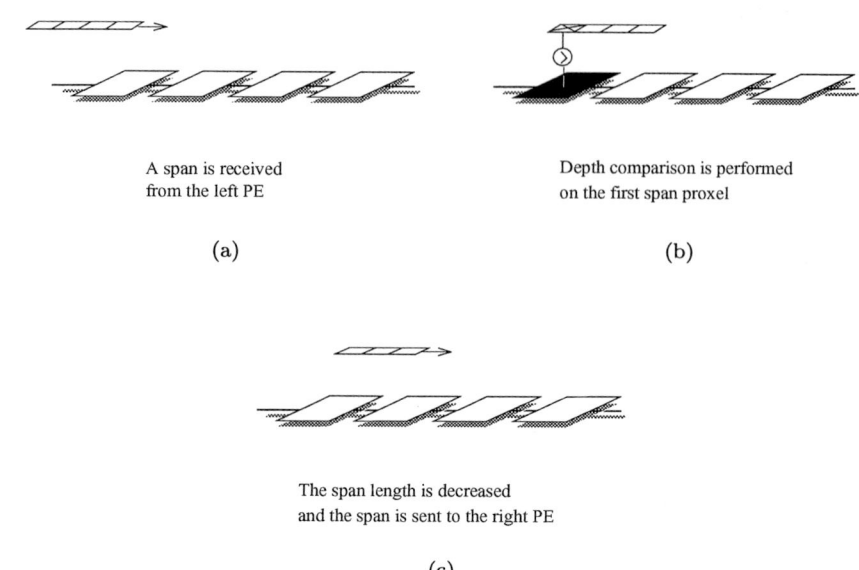

A span is received   Depth comparison is performed
from the left PE   on the first span proxel

(a)   (b)

The span length is decreased
and the span is sent to the right PE

(c)

Fig. 3. Span propagation for depth-buffering.

- A span is now stored on the PE managing its first pixel. Depth buffer can be applied for this pixel.
- The span length is then decreased from one pixel, and the span is sent to the right-side PE.
- A PE receiving a span from its left neighbor tests if the span length is not null. Otherwise, it takes a new span from its own list.
- The steps are applied again for the current span, until there is no more stored spans for any PE (detected via a flag-reduction).

This algorithm is applied simultaneously for all the PEs. This allows to depth-buffer a very high number (up to $N \times N$) of spans at the same time. Furthermore, cyclic pixel distribution provides a good load-balancing, allowing to use the Xnet for a very regular communication pattern. This load-balancing would be much more difficult to reach using a pixel block distribution scheme, as each PE would have to depth-buffer a different span length. Obviously, the number of communications is high, but measures show that they do not generate a high communication time.

4. LOCAL ILLUMINATION

Displaying a near-realistic image requires to compute some color information for each pixel where an object appears. With local illumination techniques, these information do not consider occlusions between the objects. They only take into account the sources and object locations and the view point. Illumination is built out of three components: the ambiant term (in order to provide some light to points invisible from the sources), the diffuse term (for unpolished materials) and the specular term (for bright materials). Interpolation techniques are used in order to reduce computation times. We have implemented two of these techniques: Gouraud's and Phong's interpolations.

4.1. Using Gouraud's Interpolation

Gouraud's interpolation method[12] reduces the illumination computation to the patch vertex only. During the z-buffer process, the illumination information is interpolated, in the same way the depth information is, in order to get the full local illumination. This computation is performed in the object-space, before any z-buffer operations.

With regard to our parallel z-buffer, it requires only to add some color information to the patch data-structure, to execute the illumination computation as a first process, then to add some color interpolation code.

We have run this algorithm onto four different scenes (See scene #1 and scene #3 at the end of the paper). The local illumination algorithm used is the Phong's model.[14] But as this model takes into account only pin-point sources, we are currently implementing the illumination models described by Picott in Ref. 15. Table 1 describes some average computation time per image, for different screen resolutions.

Table 1. Average computation time per image for Gouraud's interpolation.

	Scene 1 8,000 patches	Scene 2 17,000 patches	Scene 3 39,000 patches	Scene 4 100,000 patches
256×256	0.44 s	0.52 s	0.59 s	0.87 s
512×512	0.71 s	0.76 s	0.94 s	1.08 s
1024×1024	1.26 s	1.33 s	1.51 s	1.24 s

These times have been obtained by generating a sequence of 360 different images. For this purpose, the observer was set in the center of each scene, with the view direction varying from 0 to 360 degrees around a vertical axis. Only one pin-point source was used during the simulation.

These results show the efficiency of our approach: even for large databases, our approach is able to provide an illuminated image in about 1 second. But they highlight the small differences between the four scenes too: computation times are surprisingly close to each other for a given resolution. This can be explained by taking into account the size of each scene: when discretized into patches, the same patch area threshold was used for all scenes. Consequently, in all scenes, the patches have almost the same absolute size. However, the absolute sizes of each scene is very different, generating a different number patch. By setting the observer in the center of each scene, the patches appear large in the case of the first scene, but very small in the case of the last one. The number of spans and their lengths are thus large for a large projected patch, but small in the case of a small projected patch.

This provides large computation times per patch in the first case, and lower ones in the last case. As the number of patches is much higher in the most complex scene, computation times are closed from the most simple scenes. These particularity is highlighted by representing the computation times for each of the computation stages (Fig. 4).

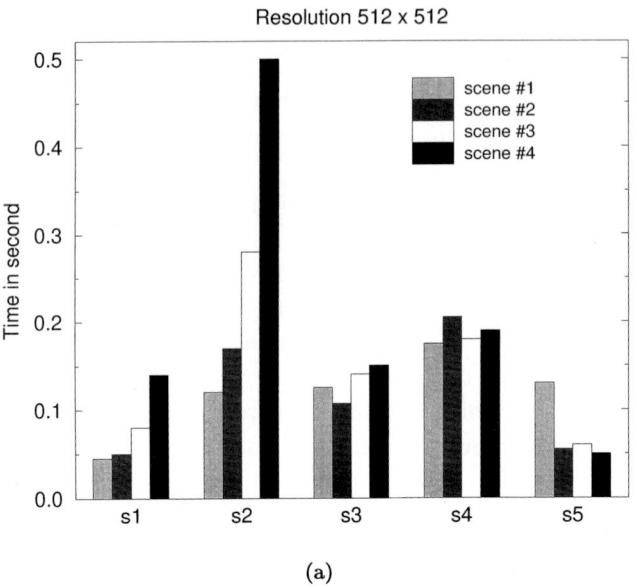

(a)

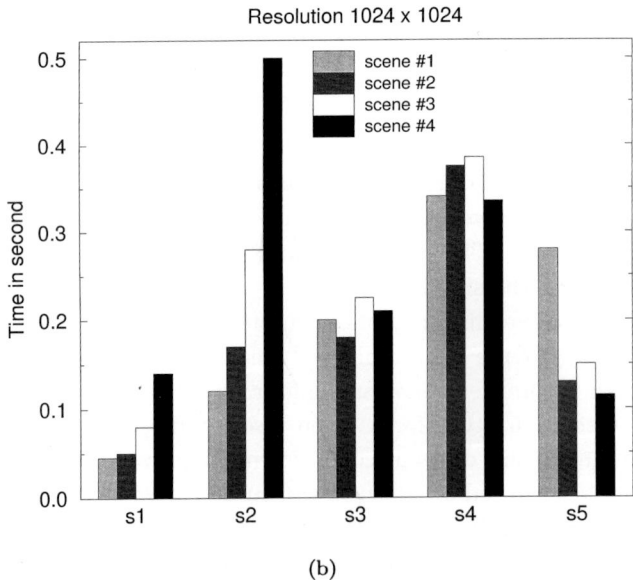

(b)

Fig. 4. Computation times distribution for two image resolutions.

The steps are represented successively: illumination of patch vertices (S_1), geometric transformations (S_2), spans generation (S_3), spans distribution (S_4) and finally depth-buffer using spans propagation (S_5). All purely computational steps increase with the number of patches, except for the span generation step (S_3): this is the direct consequence of the projected patch size, as explained above. For the same reason, the span distribution process takes the same time for the four scenes: when projected patches are large, the number of spans is high and reciprocally; as the number of patches increases, the total number of spans for the four scenes is almost the same. Furthermore, the length of small projected patches (i.e. scene #4) is lower than the one for large projected patches (i.e. scene #1). This appears during the depth buffer step where the computation time is smaller in the first scene than in the fourth one. Note the high cost of the geometric stage, that comes mainly from the clipping computation, and the growth of span distribution step with the increase of the resolution.

4.2. Using Phong's Interpolation

Phong's interpolation approach is different from the previous one. In order to compute more precisely the specular component, Phong interpolates the normals, rather than colors. The normals are known in each patch vertex; during the depth-buffer, normal in each pixel is interpolated. Once the z-buffer has been applied, each pixel contains some information about the visible object: 3D coordinates of the object visible point, normal in this point, ... All these information allow to apply a local illumination computation in each pixel. As opposed with Gouraud's approach, the illumination is implemented here as a post-z-buffer process.

Phong's interpolation is currently developed, using the SIMD z-buffer we have presented. It appears that this post process is very well-suited to a SIMD implementation, as all the PEs apply the same illumination computation. Performances however should be lower compared to the Gouraud's interpolation ones, as the interpolations are more complex, and much more illumination computation have to be performed (one per pixel, rather than one per vertex).

5. RADIOSITY FOR GLOBAL ILLUMINATION

5.1. Sequential Radiosity

Radiosity approaches require to compute geometric quantities known as *form factors*. The form factor between two patches i and j, denoted F_{ij}, represents the part of the energy diffused by patch i and reaching patch j. Computation of all form factors involves the application of a hidden-part removal algorithm for each emitting patch. Two main techniques have been proposed for this purpose:

- For projective approaches,[5,16,21,23] a projection surface is applied above an emitting patch. This surface is cut into several square samples, so called *proxel* (for projection element). All the patches are projected onto this surface, and a depth-buffer operation is applied in each covered proxel. An *elementary form-factor* (eff) is associated to each proxel. Form-factor between the emitting patch and a patch i is then approximated by adding the effs of the proxels covered by this patch. Radiosity updates are then performed and a new emitting patch is chosen.

- Some other approaches use ray-casting[26] for hidden-part removal. On one hand, rays are cast from each patch vertex to the emitting patch. Radiosity is then deduced along rays that reach the patch. On the other hand, rays are cast through the proxels of a projection surface applied onto the emitting patch. Note that this last approach can be considered as a projective approach.

Cohen[6] introduced the progressive radiosity in order to provide some kind of interactivity: by computing successively emissions from the most energetic patches, intermediate images can be displayed, even if all the interactions have not been performed yet. But progressive radiosity algorithms stay time and resource consuming, as global illumination still requires a large number of emissions. Reducing the computation time is an important area of research for radiosity, especially radiosity parallelisation. Before describing the use of our SIMD z-buffer for parallel radiosity, we summarize some of this work in the next paragraph.

5.2. Parallel Progressive Radiosity

The progressive radiosity approach offers three different levels for parallelisation:

- Several emissions are computed at the same time, each one from a different emitting patch, according to the number of available processors.[3,4,8,13,16]
- Only one emission is computed, by distributing the involved computations between the processors.[22]
- The processors collaborate for computing the form factor between the shooting patch and a given patch.[1] Note however that this approach only occurs for projective methods.

All these levels have been exploited both on MIMD and SIMD architecture. MIMD parallelisation has mainly focused on the first two levels. Differences between implementations proceed from the form factor algorithm, the network topology and the duplication/distribution/share schemes of the database. It appears however that as the database size grows, the patches have to be distributed between the processors. This distribution involves a very high number of communications, and the efficiency of these approaches decreases rapidly when the number of processors increases.[10]

5.3. Overview of SIMD Parallel Radiosity

SIMD machines require all the processors to perform the same instruction at the same time. This centralized control requires to use data parallelism, and to take care of the load-balancing between the processors. The processors are generally organized as an array, which is close to the projection plane organization used in projective methods. Consequently, several approaches have been proposed for this kind of form factor computation algorithms. In Ref. 17 we proposed to exploit the third level of parallelism we described, by projecting successively each patch onto the sampling surface. Each proxel is handled by a processor, which computes whether the projected patch is inside or outside the proxel, and applies the depth-buffer operations. However, a large number of proxels are not covered by the projected patch, and the efficiency of such an approach is small.

Varshney[25] proposed to simultaneously compute several patch projections. Each PE manages a block of neighboring proxels, and a part of the patch database. The first step of its algorithm distributes the patches to the processor managing a part of the sampling area where the patches have to be projected. Then all processors determine in which of their proxels the patches they received are visible, and apply the depth comparisons. However, the projection work is not distributed equally between the processors, as the number of patches that are visible in each sampling direction can be very different, and imbalances occur.

Parallel ray casting for form factor computation has been implemented too. Drucker[7] used a processor allocation technique for computing all the possible intersections between a ray and the voxels that lie on the way. Several rays are treated simultaneously, according to the number of available processors. However, unnecessary work is performed as all the intersections are computed along the ray path, even if an intersection exists in the first voxels. Then, the SIMD nature of the approach quickly decreases the performances when several object types are intersected onto different processors.

5.4. Using our SIMD z-Buffer

The main goal of this section is to show that the SIMD z-buffer algorithm we have developed for the MP-1 provides high speed-up in computing progressive radiosity emissions, and ensures a good balance of work between the processors.

5.4.1. Hypothesis

We suppose that form factors are approximated using a single projection plane. It is large enough to diffuse more than 95% for the emitting patch energy, and discretized uniformly into square proxels. Note that our approach can be easily extended to multilevel proxel grids[16] or to rectangular proxels.[21]

Using such a projective approach, it is obvious that the parallel z-buffer we have described does fit for the form factors computation; the computation involved for hidden-part removal are exactly the same, except for the information propagated during the z-buffer step: we do not use here a color information, but a patch identity number. However, a radiosity emission requires some additional operations, in order to compute effectively the form factors, and to distribute the energy between the patches.

5.4.2. Form factors computation

Once all the patches have been projected, each proxel encloses the identity of the patch that is visible in it. However, this visibility information can not be used

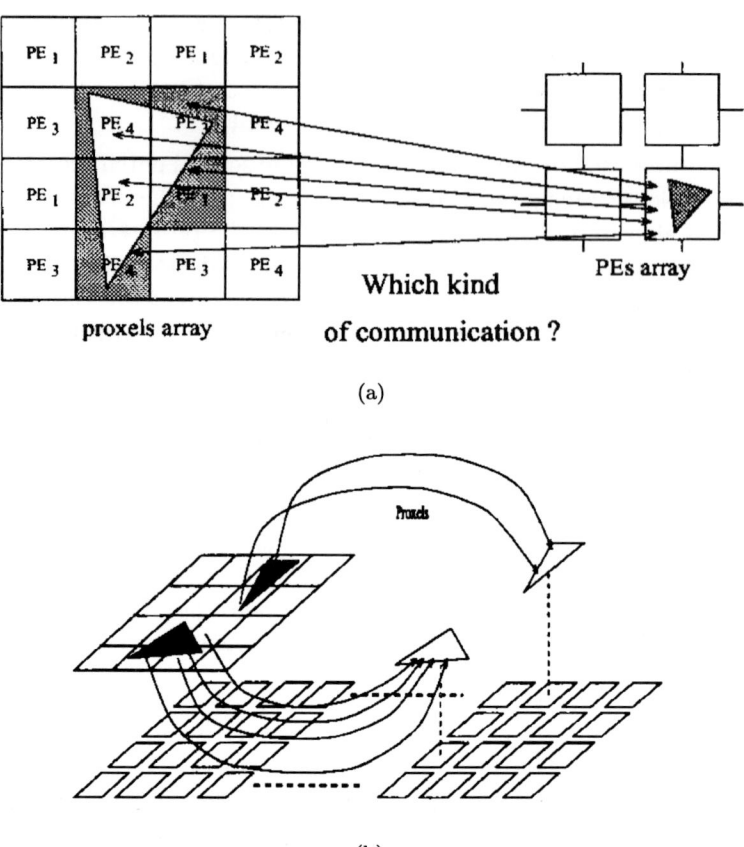

Fig. 5. (a) Distribution of proxels and patches. (b) Moving the proxels using the GR.

directly by the PE managing the proxel, as the visible patch is not necessarily managed by the same PE. See for example Fig. 5.

The gray patch projection covers several proxels, distributed across the 2 × 2 network. Each of the four PEs has one or more proxels where the patch appears. Reciprocally, the geometry and energy of this patch are managed by only one PE (here PE_4). Consequently, communications are necessary in order to associate a patch form factor with the elementary form factors of the proxels it covers.

Several communications schemes have been studied, using either the Xnet or the Global Router,[18,19] and by moving either proxels or patches. The results show that the best way to associate a patch with its eff is to send them to the corresponding patch, via the global router. The main reasons are, first, the communications do not follow a regular pattern (global router), and second the proxels can compute the PE identity that manages their patch (moving the proxels).

However, the communication time is still important, for two main reasons: on one hand, the number of proxels to send is very high, even for a low resolution. On the other hand, some hardware and software conflicts appear when using the GR.

Indeed PEs are grouped into 4×4 clusters, in order to decrease the communication hardware complexity. Each cluster has only one access to the G.R. Access to the G.R. are consequently sequential for each PE of a cluster, both for input and output. Then a PE can only receive one communication at a time. As several proxels are generally covered by a projected patch, they can not be sent simultaneously to the PE that manages the patch they "see".

Several solutions have been studied in Ref. 20 for decreasing both the number of communications and reducing the software conflicts. For the first kind of problem, a solution based on the collection of the proxels lying on the same line and containing the same projected patch, has been developed. It allows to send only one elementary form factor per span, rather than L (L being the length of the span). Then mixing functions have been studied in order to reduce the cases where several PEs want to send a proxel to the same PE. Using these two techniques, the communication time for form factors is decreased by a factor 30 to 60, according to the scene and the projection plane resolution.

5.4.3. Radiosity updates

Radiosity update is performed easily using the form factors and the emitting patch radiosity: as the patches are distributed across the PEs, each simultaneously updates its own patches radiosity. Then, a PE selects it own most energetic patch, and a reduction operation is performed amongst all those potentially new emitting patches, in order to find the most energetic one. All these operations are performed efficiently on the MP-1, as they require the same amount of computation.

5.5. Some Results

This algorithm has been applied onto a 16 K PEs MP-1, using the same four databases used for local illumination. The measures are concerned with the average computation time per emission and the distribution of the computational effort between the different steps of the algorithm. The average computation time per emission is presented in Table 2, for 3 different projection plane resolutions (resolution N means that the projection plane has been cut into $N \times N$ proxels).

Remember that these times are only for a unique emission, and that several emissions are required before radiosity convergence can be obtained. The same sequential radiosity algorithm has been run on a sequential machine, in order to compare the performances between the sequential and parallel machines. The sequential machine is a SUN Sparc LX workstation, that provides about 4.6 MFlops.

These results highlight the high speed-up obtained with our approach, either for small or complex databases. Speed-up is more important for complex databases, as data-parallelism is more efficient in these cases.

In the same way that the results presented for image display, computation times are similar for high resolutions. The same explanation is given: as the database complexity increases, the projected patch size decreases. Consequently, for our 4 databases, the total number of generated spans is still the same. This appears

Table 2. Average computation times per shooting step.

	Scene 1 8,000 patches	Scene 2 17,000 patches	Scene 3 39,000 patches	Scene 4 100,000 patches
	resolution 256 × 256			
sequential	7.2 s	14.8 s	28.5 s	63.2 s
MP-1	0.296 s	0.371 s	0.551 s	0.668 s
	resolution 512 × 512			
sequential	16.5 s	25.3 s	49.1 s	81.6 s
MP-1	0.524 s	0.540 s	0.692 s	0.815 s
	resolution 1024 × 1024			
sequential	37.4 s	51.9 s	66.5 s	92.7 s
MP-1	1.183 s	1.073 s	1.175 s	1.283 s

in Fig. 6, which describes the computation times distribution, according to each algorithm step.

The steps that appear in this figure are the geometric transformations (S_1), the spans computation (S_2), the spans distribution (S_3), the depth-buffer (S_4) and the radiosity update (S_5). When the resolution increases, the computation time of all the steps using spans increase. This growth is not as regular as the times in Fig. 4. In case of radiosity computation, projection plane is not applied in the center of the scene, but onto different emitting patches. These ones are first on walls (windows) and ceilings (light sources). Then reflexions are computed from different

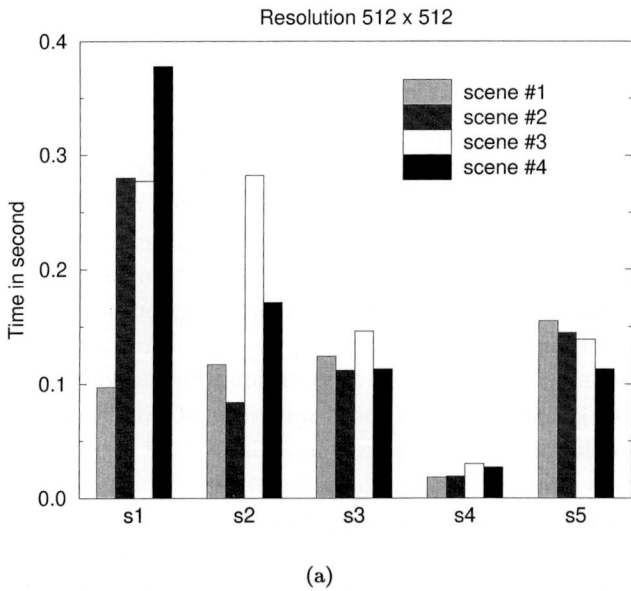

(a)

Fig. 6. Computation times distribution for two projection plane resolutions.

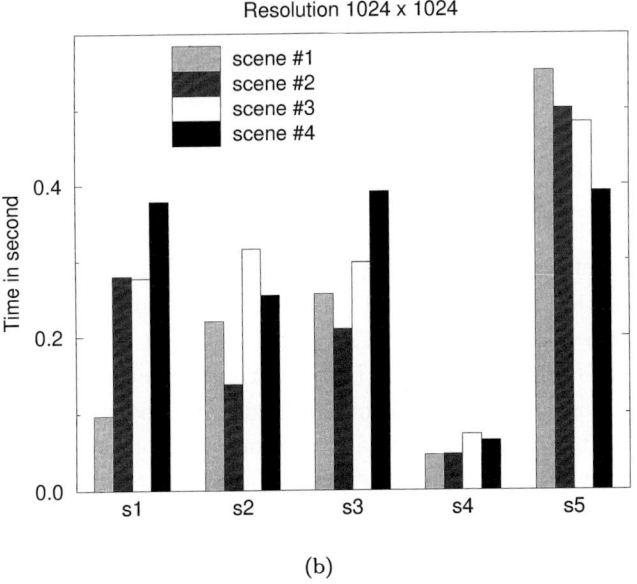

(b)

Fig. 6. (*Cont'd*).

A view of two databases

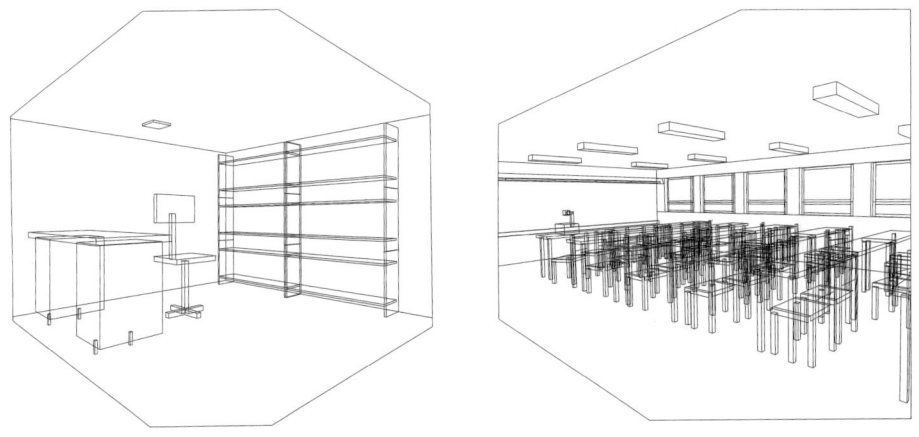

Fig. 7. Wireframe views of scene #1 (left part) and scene #3 (right part).

objects lying inside the scene. Consequently, computation is not so regular as for the display process script. Note the very large part taken by the last step, which is concerned with the eff communications. As previously described, the number of proxels to exchange is very high, and the number of conflicts grows with the resolution.

6. CONCLUSION AND PERSPECTIVES

This paper presents a new massively parallel approach for the well-known z-buffer hidden-part removal algorithm. It is implemented onto the MP-1 SIMD massively parallel computer. Our approach provides efficient use of the PEs capabilities and well-balanced computation, by splitting the sequential algorithm into successive stages. Each of them is developed by taking care to use efficiently the SIMD control of the target architecture. This efficiency has been proved with the use of this algorithm in cost effective local and global illumination approaches.

Local illumination is implemented using Phong's illumination model and Gouraud's color interpolation method. This provides rapid images even for complex databases. Phong's interpolation method is currently developed.

The reliability of our algorithm is highlighted by its use in a progressive radiosity method. It allows to reduce dramatically the computation of each form factor computation step, providing a very high speed-up as compared to the same sequential algorithm. Furthermore, as displaying radiosity image requires Gouraud's interpolation method, it is easy to display intermediate images from the MP-1 during the radiosities computation.

Several new developments are studied today. For local illumination approaches, it could be interesting to implement some texture mapping methods. Approaches based on bump mapping seem easy to add to the Phong's normal interpolation. However some other approaches, like picture mapping, are more difficult to implement on a SIMD parallel computer. Aliasing occurs in all computer-generated images. Oversampling in each pixel can reduce the aliasing, but the computation time grows with the number of subpixels. We are today studying some less expensive methods. The radiosity implementation is actually based on a large single projection plane. However some loss of energy occurs for the grazing directions; furthermore accuracy in form factor approximation requires a high number of proxels, especially when the database complexity increases. We are working on the implementation of a disk projection surface, based on the Nusselt's equivalent. This kind of projection surface involves more complex computation, but it eliminates the energy loss, and reduces considerably the number of proxels.

REFERENCES

1. D. R. Baum and J. M. Winget, "Real time radiosity through parallel processing and hardware acceleration", *Comput. Graphics* **25**, 4 (1991) 51–60.
2. E. Catmull, "Computer display of curved surfaces", *Proc. IEEE Conf. Computer Graphics Pattern Recognition Data Structures*, May 1975, pp. 11.
3. A. G. Chalmers and D. J. Paddon, "Parallel processing of progressive refinement radiosity methods", *Second Eurographics Workshop on Rendering*, Barcelona, May 1991.
4. S. E. Chen, "A progressive radiosity method and its implementation in a distributed processing environment", Master's Thesis, Cornell University, Ithaca, USA, Jan 1989.
5. M. F. Cohen and D. P. Greenberg, "The hemicube: A radiosity solution for complex environments", *Comput. Graphics* **19**, 3 (1985) 31–40.

6. M. F. Cohen, S. E. Chen, J. R. Wallace and D. P. Greenberg, "A progressive refinement approach to fast radiosity image generation", *Comput. Graphics* **22**, 4 (1988) 75–84.

7. S. M. Drucker and P. Schröder, "Fast radiosity using a data parallel architecture", *Third Eurographics Workshop on Rendering*, Bristol, May 1992, 247–258.

8. M. Feda and W. Purgathofer, "Progressive refinement radiosity on a transputer network", *Second Eurographics Workshop on Rendering*, Barcelona, May 1991.

9. H. Fuchs *et al.*, "Pixel-planes 5: A heterogeneous multiprocessor graphics system using processor-enhanced memories", *Comput. Graphics* **23**, 3 (1989) 79–88.

10. P. Guitton, J. Roman and G. Subrenat, "Implementation results and analysis of a parallel progressive radiosity", *Proc. IEEE/ACM 1995 Parallel Rendering Symposium'95*, Al Paula, October 1995.

11. C. M. Goral, K. E. Torrance and D. P. Greenberg, "Modeling the interaction of light between diffuse surfaces", *SIGGRAPH 84* **23**, 3 (1989) 213–222.

12. H. Gouraud, "Continuous shading of curved surfaces", *IEEE Trans. Comput.* **20**, 6 (1971) 623–629.

13. P. Guitton, J. Roman and C. Schlick, "Two parallel approaches for progressive radiosity", *Second Eurographics Workshop on Rendering*, Barcelona, May 1991.

14. B. T. Phong, "Illumination for computer generated pictures", *Commun. ACM* **18**, 6 (1975).

15. K. P. Picott, "Extensions of the linear and area lighting models", *IEEE Comput. Graphics Appl.* (1992) 31–38.

16. R. J. Recker, D. W. George and D. P. Greenberg, "Acceleration techniques for progressive refinement radiosity", *Comput. Graphics* **24**, 2 (1990) 59–66.

17. C. Renaud, F. Bricout and E. Leprêtre, "Hemispherical projection for progressive radiosity calculation on massively parallel architectures", *Eighth Eurographics Workshop on Graphics Hardware*, Barcelona, September 1993.

18. C. Renaud, "Approaches parallèles pour la radiosité", Ph.D. Thesis, University of Lille, October 1993.

19. C. Renaud, F. Bricout and E. Leprêtre, "An object parallel approach for radiosity on the MP-1", *Int. Conf. Massively Parallel Processing Applications and Developments*, Delft, June 21–23, 1994, pp. 887–894.

20. C. Renaud, "Reducing communications for massively parallel radiosity on the MP-1", Technical Report, Laboratoire d'Informatique du Littoral, to be published.

21. F. Sillion and C. Puech, "A general two-pass method integrating specular and diffuse reflection", *Comput. Graphics* **23**, 3 (1989) 335–344.

22. D. B. Singh, S. G. Abraham and F. H. Westervelt, "Computing radiosity solution on a high performances workstation LAN", *First High Performance Distributed Comp.*, N.Y. September 1992, pp. 248–257.

23. S. N. Spencer, "The hemisphere radiosity method: A tale of two algorithms", *Eurographics Workshop on Photosimulation, Realism and Physics in Computer Graphics*, Rennes June 1990, pp. 127–135.

24. T. Théoharis and I. Page, "Parallel incremental polygon rendering on a SIMD processor array", *Parallel Processing Computer Vision and Display*, pp. 329–337.

25. A. Varshney and J. F. Prins, "An environment-projection approach to radiosity for mesh connected computers", *Third Eurographics Workshop on Rendering*, Bristol, May 1992, pp. 271–281.

26. J. R. Wallace, K. A. Elmquist and E. A. Haines, "A ray tracing algorithm for progressive radiosity", *Comput. Graphics* **23**, 3 (1989) 315–324.

C. Renaud received his Ph.D. degree in computer science in 1993, from the University of Lille (France). He is currently assistant professor of computer science in the University of Littoral (Calais, France).

His research includes realistic image synthesis, mathematics and parallelism in computer graphics.

A LOAD BALANCED PARALLEL GROUND VISUALIZATION TOOL

SYLVAIN CONTASSOT-VIVIER

Ecole Normale Supérieure de Lyon
Laboratoire de l'Informatique du Parallélisme
46 Allée d'Italie, 69364 Lyon cedex 07, France.
scontass@{ lip.ens-lyon.fr, eric.univ-lyon2.fr}

We propose in this paper, a parallel implementation of a ground visualization algorithm. Our input data consist in a Digital Elevation Model (DEM) covering a rectangular region, together with a raster image of the same area (the texture). The goal of the algorithm is to compute in parallel, images of the DEM from any point of view while mapping the texture onto the surface. The main originality of our approach concerns the distribution of the data, leading to a load-balanced and scalable parallel algorithm. We use a workload estimation to partition the output image, and then redistribute the input data according to this division. Special attention is paid on the data structures used for minimizing the cost of communications.

Keywords: Parallelism, 3D visualization, texture-mapping, load balancing, data repartition.

1. INTRODUCTION

In geology, 3D visualization of texture-mapped grounds is an important tool for scientists. Researchers need to visualize interactively the images of grounds from any angle, and to make measurements such as altitude reading, contour levels tracing, curvature or slope computations, etc. To fulfill these needs, we have designed the *Volter* (for *surVOL de TERrain* = ground flying over) software that includes an interactive module as well as an animation engine. Moreover, this application could easily be integrated in a GIS[a] in order to visualize different types of information in a 3D representation of a given ground. The only constraint would be to convert these informations in a texture format, that is to say, in a raster image. In this case, the main interest would be the interactivity and the ability to directly extract information of a GIS from a 3D visualization of a ground.

Yet, the common huge size of actual data is not compatible, in a sequential programming model, with real time computation rates. SPOT images typically present a resolution of 6000×6000 pixels.

The goal of the study presented here is to parallelize the computation of these images in order to minimize the response time of the system. We have used the *PPCM*[b] library, developed in the LIP laboratory. This library allows the use of several MIMD distributed memory machines in a portable way.

---

[a]Geographical Information System
[b]Parallel Portable Communication Module

Parallel Image Analysis: Tools and Models (1998) 91–105
© World Scientific Publishing Company

The paper is organized as follows: Sec. 2 presents different possible strategies used in the literature for the parallelization of general visualization techniques. Section 3 gives more details on the specific data structure we use for textured ground representation, as well as on the sequential algorithm we employ for texture mapping. We explain our parallelization scheme of this algorithm in Sec. 4, and give results on its performances in Sec. 5. Finally, we discuss in Sec. 6 some possible improvements of this parallel algorithm, including the handling of frame-to-frame coherence and multiresolution techniques.

2. PARALLEL VISUALIZATION TECHNIQUES

When dealing with computer graphics, we classically have to handle two distinct spaces, namely object space (the scene to visualize), and image space (the screen where the scene has to be represented).

These two sets of data can lead to three major parallelization schemes, depending on which space is decomposed (object, image or both).

2.1. Object Space Division

There are several ways to divide object spaces. The main idea is to divide the scene into disjoint subsets and to let each processor handle the contribution of its subset to the whole image. The fact that the processing of polygons can be decomposed into independent steps makes it possible to use hardware or software pipelines. A second level of parallelism is achieved by using several independent pipelines.[7,8]

Two problems occur with these techniques. The first one is that the pipeline's rate is limited by the slowest stage which represents a potential loss of efficiency. The second (and most important) problem is the bottleneck created by the concurrent access to the frame buffer. Image composition-trees have been proposed to solve this problem, but this approach is limited to a few number of processors.

2.2. Image Space Division

As for the object space, there are several ways to divide the image space. We can proceed by working over the pixels or groups of pixels. These methods are the most used and have been the subject of many studies.[10,12,15] The most appropriate techniques for a software issue are those which associate groups of adjacent pixels (horizontal or vertical strips or rectangles) to elementary processors.

The main problem with this approach concerns the distribution of the scene. If it is duplicated to all the local memories of the processors, redundant computations occur, leading to a non-scalable solution. Partial duplication of the scene is possible, but leads to important communication overheads. Some algorithms were made to minimize the communications by statically distributing the data as in Ref. 2, but they were confronted with the problem of load imbalance. Whelan[14] and Roble[13] tried to solve this problem by using a static decomposition taking into account the load balance.

The grouping of adjacent pixels to a same processor allows to take advantage of spatial coherence when rendering objects. On the other hand, it can suffer from load balancing problems, since some regions can be dramatically more loaded than others. The bloc-cyclic allocation of image data can be used to find a compromise between balancing the load and exploiting coherence.

Finally, there is another method which is based on the parallel drawing of each polygon,[1,9] there are more constraints and parallelism is limited. Again, performances are restricted by synchronization or access conflicts problems.

2.3. Conclusion

Our bibliographical study has enabled to emphasize some important criteria for a good parallel visualization algorithm. They are:

- Granularity (size of tasks),
- Load balancing,
- Data distribution and access (memory management, ...),
- Use of coherence,
- Scalability.

We could observe in the literature that no algorithm can at present, satisfy all the criteria listed above — maybe because it is not really possible. The goal of our study is to try to solve several of these issues in the particular case of texture-mapped grounds.

2.4. Hybrid Object and Image Division

Due to their lack of scalability, image-space only and object-space only solutions are unusable for large scenes and important frame-buffer resolutions. We proposed in a previous study a two-steps algorithm based on a mixed approach.[4] The objects are first geometrically transformed in parallel to the screen coordinates, allowing to compute a load estimation of each row of the image. A strip-wise partition is then computed according to this estimation, so that the workload is well balanced among each region. The scene is then reshuffled according to this new image partition, and the sequential algorithm can then be applied on each subregion.

3. SEQUENTIAL VISUALIZATION OF DEMs

The texture-mapped grounds are composed of two input data structures. On one hand, we have a Digital Elevation Model (DEM), organized as an orthogonal mesh of points whose altitudes are given (see Fig. 1).

On the other hand, a raster image, representing the texture of the ground, that can be superimposed to the DEM. The number of points in the texture has typically a factor of one to ten times more than in the DEM, in each dimension. Each grid point of the DEM can be associated to a corresponding position in the texture image. A usual way to visualize the textured ground is to decompose the DEM into triangles which are scanned sequentially. Each triangle is then colored according to

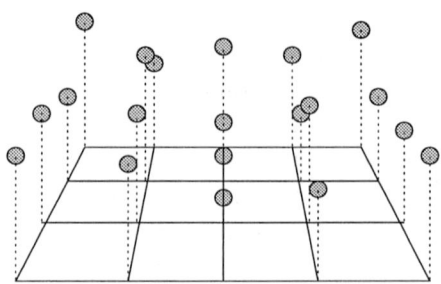

Fig. 1. Digital Elevation Model.

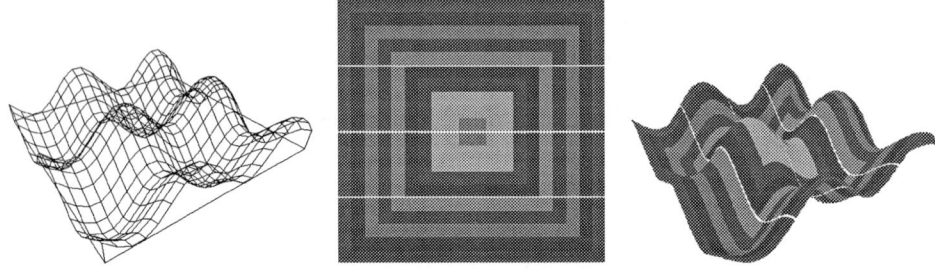

Fig. 2. Example of visualization (right) starting from a DEM (left) and a texture image (middle).

the texture coordinates of its inner points, that are interpolated from the texture coordinates of its three vertices. A more detailed study over this technique can be found in Ref. 5. Figure 2 shows a synthetic example where a square texture is mapped onto a sinusoidal surface.

4. PARALLEL ALGORITHM

According to our bibliographical study, we chose a hybrid object and image based method similar to the one used in Ref. 4. The main originality of this new algorithm consists in the data structures used for the scene representation, and for interprocessor communications. But before entering into details, we first explain how the data are initially allocated, and give some hints on our load balancing strategy.

4.1. Load Balancing

In the following, we assume that we have a p processors distributed memory machine, where processors are numbered from 0 to $p - 1$.

The DEM is initially distributed using a strip-wise subdivision. Like in Ref. 4, we estimate the workload associated to a given row of the picture, by counting the number of polygons intersecting this row. Each processor does this computation for the portion of DEM it has been allocated. All the local information are then aggregated (but not centralized) by a parallel reduction operation. An irregular strip-wise partition of the image is then computed, such that the load of each strip is approximately constant. We use the "Elastic" load balancing scheme introduced in Ref. 11 for computing this new partition.

In Fig. 3 can be seen the partition into four strips (4 processors) for a DEM of Mars.[c] The white lines represent the frontiers between the strips.

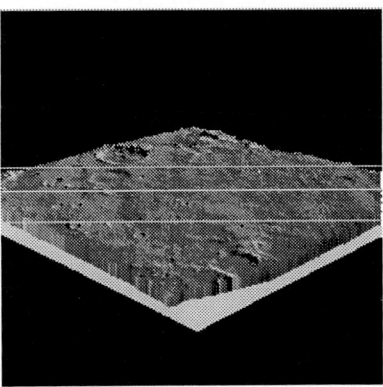

Fig. 3.   Division in four strips of a Mars DEM.

In the following section, we explain the data structure we use for interprocessor communications. Assume first that the texture is duplicated in all the local memories of the processors. We show in Sec. 4.3 how to remove this constraint.

4.2.   Redistribution of the DEM

Once the image is partitioned, the DEM has to be redistributed among the processors according to the subdivision of the screen. In order to save memory and communication time, we want to send to a given processor, only the data it will need to perform its rendering.

A first solution would be to represent explicitly the polygons, and to use the communication scheme employed in Ref. 4 for general polygon-based scenes. Nevertheless, this would amount to very large messages since we would loose the compactness of the DEM representation of the surface. Thus, we chose to redistribute DEM points themselves in a much more compact data-structure, allowing nevertheless the receiver of the message to rebuild triangles.

Each processor computes p buckets for the p possible destinations of the DEM points it owns initially. A DEM point goes into bucket q if its projection falls into subregion q of the image. Additionally some points need to be added to bucket q to allow processor q to reconstitute the triangles overlapping frontiers of region q.

In Fig. 4, on the left, the chosen triangulation of the DEM and the points added to a single vertex can be seen. On the right are represented the points added

---

[c]Courtesy of the Science of Earth Department of the ENS Lyon

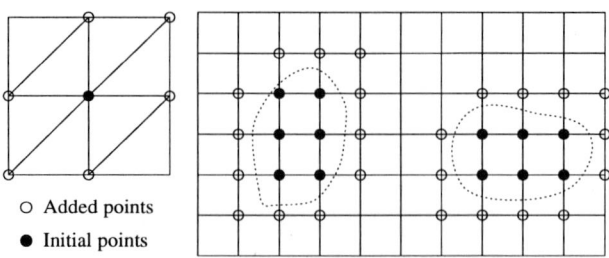

Fig. 4. Triangulation of the DEM and points added to a single DEM vertex (left) and to a general set of DEM vertices (right).

to a general subset of the DEM. It is important to note that depending on the topography of the surface, the set of DEM points that are sent to a given processor might form several connected regions.

Two neighboring DEM points have a high probability to be projected into the same subregion. This remark makes it possible to code efficiently the message that a processor will send to another one.

A compact structure has to be constructed in order to communicate all the data in a single message. We use for this purpose the regular grid structure of the DEM. The set of DEM points that were inserted into the same bucket, is decomposed into a set of horizontal segments. In the example of Fig. 4 (right hand-side), the set of points is coded with 9 horizontal segments. The message between two processors includes thus the following data: the total number of segments that have to be sent, and then the list of segments. For each segment, we include the number of points that compose it, the position of the first point in the grid of the DEM (x and y), and the list of the image coordinates (X, Y and Z) of each point in the segment. The coordinates of the points are given in the image space (which increases the size of the messages) to avoid to reproject them, since it is more time consuming on our target machines than having longer messages. The two times we had to compare were on one side about 25 floating-point operations for the reprojection of a point, and on the other side, the communication of 8 additional bytes of data (three floats instead of one). This choice was made after the test of both strategies.

Finally, once the data of the DEM are reshuffled by a so-called *multi-scattering* all-to-all communication, the visualization can be done, restricting the draw space to the strip assigned to the processor. A clever scanning of the segments is used to reconstruct the triangles efficiently, refer to Ref. 6 for more details.

We assumed in this section that the texture was duplicated in all the local memories of the processors. If it is not possible because of memory constraints, we use a similar mechanism as for the DEM distribution, as described in the following section.

4.3. Distribution of the Texture

To map the texture onto the ground, each processor must have at least the piece of texture corresponding to the piece of DEM it owns. The information collected while constructing the DEM's messages are used to build the ones of the texture. Thus, the messages have the same structure as before except that in place of the image coordinates of the points, there are the pixels' colors of the texture. Since the texture image can be at a higher resolution than the DEM, the number of segments may be larger.

Once the texture is shared out, we have to retrieve a given pixel from its absolute coordinates in the texture image, since these are used for the mapping. The pixels are placed in a linear array. We use a reference table which contains the information about each segment (position in the texture and number of pixels) and their places in the array. So, to retrieve a pixel, we find the segment containing it in the reference table, and then, we can get it in the array.

Using such a reference table creates a small overhead. Nevertheless, the search time of the right segment can be accelerated by bucket sorting the segments in the reference table by y-coordinate, and beginning the search with the last segment used. Indeed, when drawing a triangle, the pixels of texture that are used consecutively are often very close to each other.

5. RESULTS

The first paragraph of this section shortly presents the PPCM library used to implement our parallel algorithm. In the scope of our study, its main interesting feature is the portability over several parallel machines. Most of our results are obtained on a *Volvox* machine and a *Cray T3D*. The Volvox is designed by Archipel, whose nodes include a i860 processor for the computations and a T800 Transputer for the communications. The Cray T3D[d] machine uses DEC Alpha processors and presents better absolute performances than the Volvox.

The data used for our experiments are a DEM with a size of 700×680 points and a texture which is a 8 bits image of the same size (in pixels). These relatively small input data are imposed by the small amount of memory available on each node of the parallel machines. Since we want to compare the parallel execution time to the time on one node, the whole dataset has to fit into the memory of a single node.

5.1. PPCM

In this section, we don't attempt to detail PPCM but just point out its main features and its organization. For more details on PPCM, the reader should refer to Ref. 3.

PPCM is a C library which provides a set of communication and load balancing procedures. Concerning the load balancing, there is a set of routines that facilitates the workload computation and the rearrangement of the data. For example, the elastic algorithm used to compute the image partition in our algorithm is implemented in PPCM.

Most of the common communication types are provided. One to one, one to all, all to one and all to all communication routines are implemented.

---

[d] Access granted by the CEA of Grenoble.

The main originality of PPCM resides in two aspects. The first one is its portability since PPCM is available on several parallel machines including iPSC, Volvox, Cray T3D, Paragon and PVM. Moreover, the way PPCM is written makes easier the portage on new machines. The second one is the virtual topologies usable for the communication routines. Since there are different interconnection networks usable to design parallel machines, several virtual topologies are available like a grid, a hypercube and a ring.

5.2. Results on the Volvox

The graphs, in Fig. 5, show the times to compute one image as a function of the number of processors, with two different sizes of the output image.

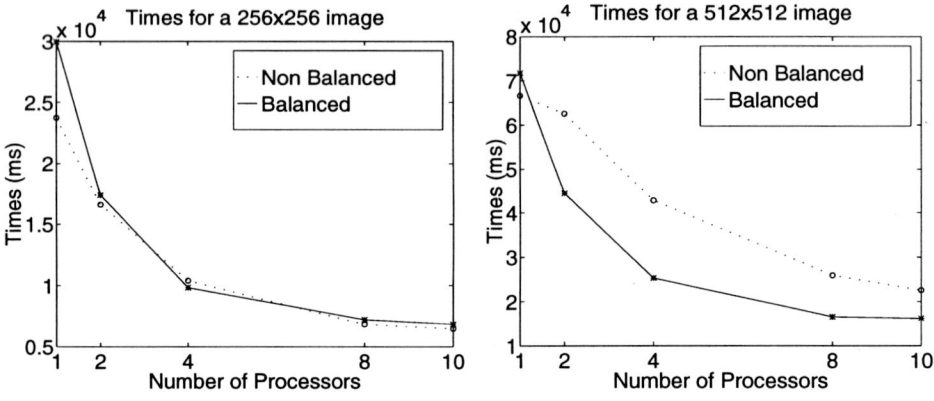

Fig. 5. Times to compute one image on a Volvox in function of the number of processors for two sizes of output images.

Two series of tests have been made for each size of output image, either using the load balancing algorithm or not (the static version consists in dividing the image into p equal sized strips). In order to emphasize the time to compute the loads, a distinction is even made with only one processor between the balanced and the static versions.

In the left graph, we observe that the non-balanced version is sometimes better than the static one. Nevertheless, in the other graph, the balanced version is always better. This difference between the two graphs is due to the influence of the size of the output image on the performances.

In Fig. 6, the time repartition of the different parts of our algorithm is given (communications, visualization, load balancing when it is relevant, ...) over each processor and for the two versions of the algorithm; using a configuration of eight processors and a 512×512 pixels output image. The effectiveness of the balancing clearly appears in the visualization times (it is the part of the algorithm we balance). We also observe that the times to compute the loads are the same over the processors and the communication times are slightly different (we can't directly supervise them

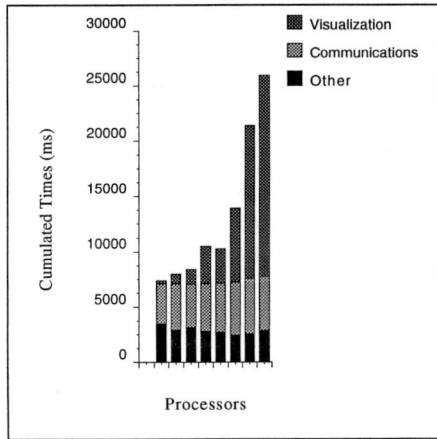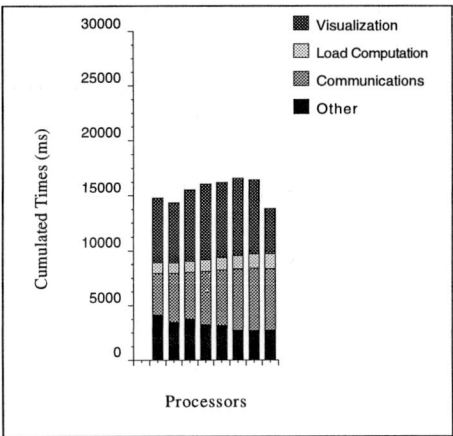

Fig. 6. Cumulated times for a 512×512 image on 8 processors of the Volvox. Static allocation (left). Dynamic Load Balancing (right).

since they rely on the data redistribution and the internal configuration of the parallel machine).

We observed in Fig. 5, that the execution time decreases when the number of processors increases (which was the purpose of the parallelization). Figure 7 illustrates the speedup of the algorithm as a function of the number of processors, both for the balanced and unbalanced version. The speedup seems to reach quickly an upper bound, but this is due to the small dataset (ground and texture) we used for our experiments, as well as the small image resolution used for rendering.

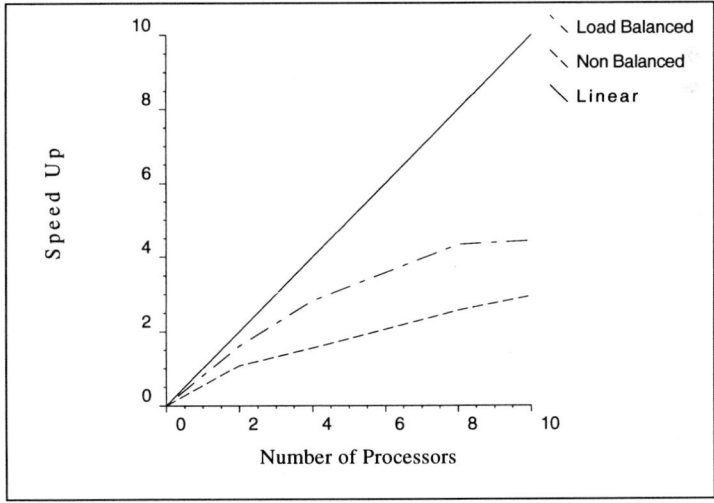

Fig. 7. Speedup with the 700 × 680 DEM in a 512 × 512 image, obtained on a Volvox.

To illustrate this dependence, we have plotted in Fig. 8, the efficiency of the parallelization as a function of the size of the output image. We clearly see that increasing the resolution of the image increases the efficiency and therefore the speedup of the algorithm.

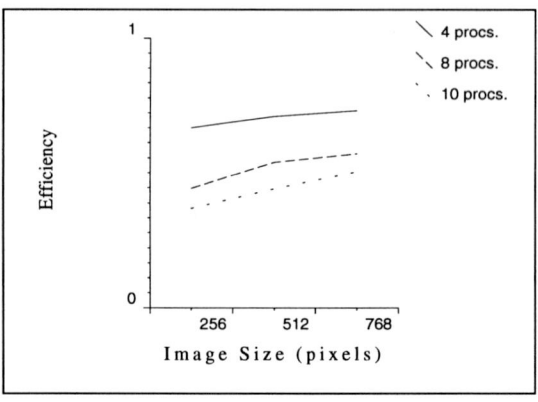

Fig. 8.   Efficiency as a function of the size of the output image, obtained on a Volvox.

This dependence can be explained by two main reasons: the first one is that smaller the output image, smaller is the visualization time. Therefore, the overheads of the parallelization take the most important part of the computations. This is why, in the first graph of Fig. 5, the non-balanced version is sometimes faster, since there is no time spent to load balance.

The second reason is the precision of the strips division. If the image is small, the projected DEM is observed smaller and more polygons are intersecting each line. The strip-wise division is therefore less accurate (it is more difficult to have the same amount of work on each strip). In the other case, the DEM is better spread on the image and the lines have less important loads; hence, it is easier to obtain an accurate division, giving a better repartition of the work.

At last, another critical parameter for the performances is the position of the observer, and more particularly his distance to the ground. Giving a DEM and the size of the output image; the closer we are to the ground, the smaller is the part we see. Thus, there are much less data to process for an equal time of visualization since the viewed triangles are bigger in the image, then covering a larger area. Consequently, there are less communications and the overheads are reduced. Figure 9 illustrates this fact by a plot of the speedup as function of the distance between the observer and the DEM; each line corresponds to a given configuration (number of processors).

So, these results obtained on the Volvox allow us to deduce some critical parameters for the effectiveness of the algorithm. Nevertheless, other experiments on a faster parallel machine with more processors would give us additional information about the behavior of our algorithm.

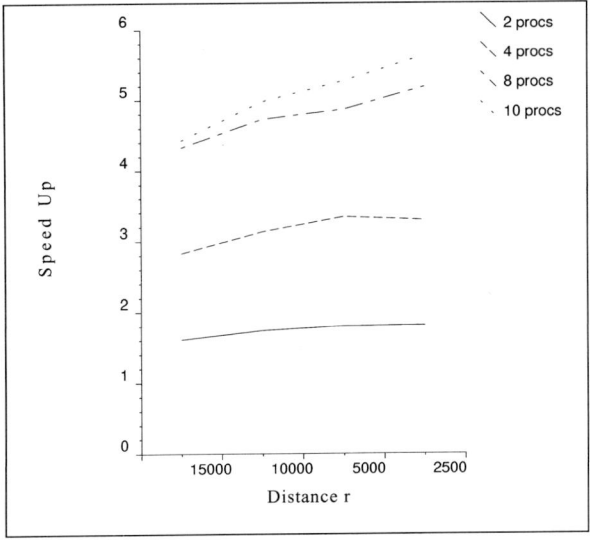

Fig. 9. Speedup evolution according to the DEM-observer distance, obtained on a Volvox.

5.3. Results on a Cray T3D

In order to have a complete experimental study, we have also used a Cray T3D machine to confirm the previous results and to observe our algorithm on a faster architecture.

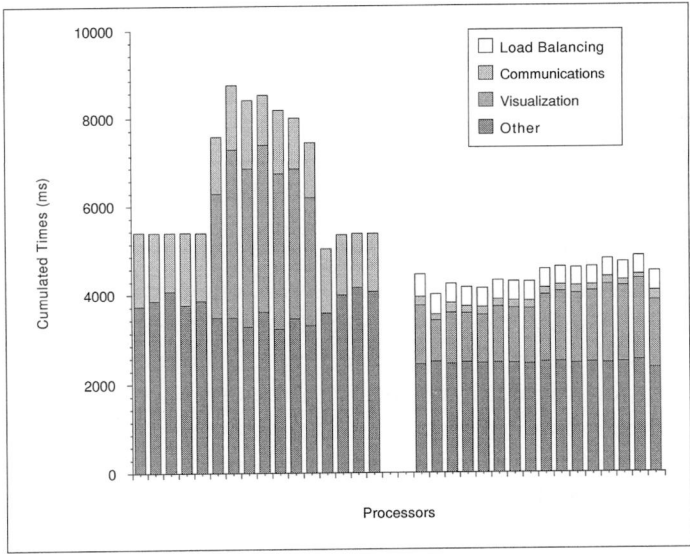

Fig. 10. Cumulated times for a 512×512 image on 16 processors of a Cray T3D. Static allocation (left). Dynamic Load Balancing (right).

In Fig. 10, cumulated times on each processor to compute a 512×512 image with 16 processors are presented. The superiority of the balanced version over the static one is clearly confirmed. The most loaded processors are not the same in Figs. 10 and 6 with the static allocation because the view angle differs between the two experiments.

Another important difference between the two versions of our algorithm, is the communication time. This time is much more important in the static version than in the balanced one. This is due to the fact that, in the static version, some processors can need much more data than the others, and thus create a bottleneck slowing down of the communications.

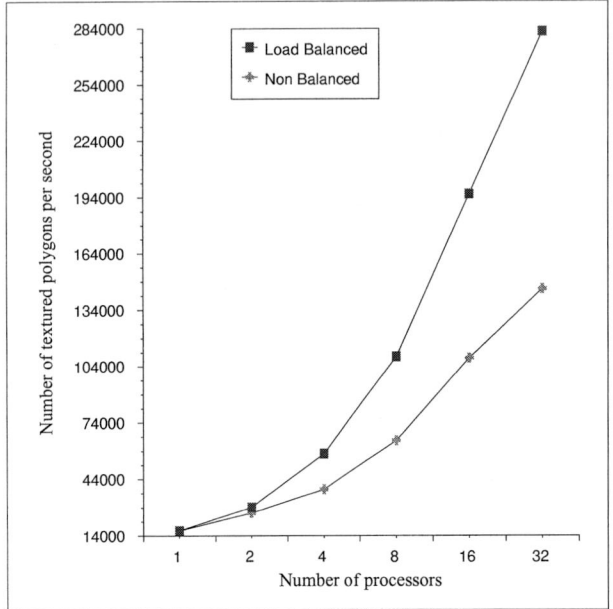

Fig. 11. Number of textured polygons computed per second in function of the number of processors used, obtained on a Cray T3D.

Finally, an interesting result we obtain is the computation rate of the textured polygons. Figure 11 shows the number of polygons processed by our parallel algorithm. We can see that even if the performances are not linearly proportional to the number of processors, they still increase with the degree of parallelism. Moreover, absolute performances are quite good considering non specialized processors, since we obtain about 280000 textured polygons per second with 32 processors. These computation rates are of the same order as current graphic workstations performances.

This ends the experimental analysis of our parallel program. The results are promising and give a good base to study various optimizations. The following part briefly gives several interesting issues for further developments.

6. POSSIBLE OPTIMIZATIONS

Although the current parallel version of our program gives good results, it is yet possible to improve it at several levels. We give here some ideas which seem interesting to study more precisely.

Multiresolution: The idea consists in taking into account only those points of the DEM which are significant enough, for instance because they are at a minimum distance of each other in the output image. Therefore, the visualization quality would be almost the same but the amount of data would be smaller, representing an important gain in time. The same approach can be used for the texture, that can be prefiltered at different resolutions.

Coherence: When computing an animation, the use of the coherence between successive images allows to avoid some computations, for instance in the workload estimation. But the most important optimization concerns the communications since the DEM's points that are needed by one processor for a given image are almost the same as the ones it had to process at the previous one. Very few new data have thus to be redistributed and most of these communications are local.

Rectangular division: One of the major problems with the strips division is the limitation of the number of processors used, especially with small images. Indeed, for a given number of processors, the rectangular division gives better results than strips one, because we can have a more precise repartition of the work. Thus, we could generalize our load balancing strategy to a rectangular subdivision while computing the loads for the rows and the columns of the image.

7. CONCLUSION

The parallel version of Volter was presented. It is based on an irregular strip-wise subdivision of the output image, leading to a balanced execution; the DEM and the texture were shared out in order to have just the necessary data on each processor. The implementation was developed under the *PPCM* environment developed at the LIP. This environment allows the use of several parallel machines like an iPSC, a Volvox, a Paragon, a network of stations (PVM), and a Cray T3D.

This study allowed us to point out the critical parameters influencing the performances of this kind of program. The most important are the size of the output image, the size of the data to visualize, and the amount of data effectively in the image (that directly depends on the observer–ground distance).

The domain of visualization often requires large computation times. In order to reach interactivity or to create animations, these times must be as small as possible. The technique presented here allows to process very large amount of data, at reasonable speed. We showed how to take into account the specific data structure of the grounds represented by DEMs. Moreover, we proposed some optimizations that should further improve our absolute performances.

The absolute performances were quite good since our algorithm was able to render 280000 polygons per second with 32 processors.

REFERENCES

1. M. Allison, private communication, July 1991.
2. P. Chang and R. Jain, "A multi-processor system for hidden surface removal", *Comput. Graphics* **15**, 4 (1981) 405–436.
3. H.-P. Charles, O. Baby, A. Fou illoux, S. Miguet, L. Perroton, Y. Robert and S. Ubéda, "Ppcm: A portable parallel communication module", Technical Report 92-04, LIP-IMAG, ENS-Lyon, 46 allée d'Italie, 69364 Lyon CEDEX 07, 1992.
4. H.-P. Charles, L. Lefevre and S. Miguet, "An optimized and load-balanced portable parallel ZBuffer", In *SPIE Symp. Electronic Imaging: Science and Technology*, 1995.
5. S. Contassot-Vivier, "Reconstruction 3D de terrains texturés", Traineeship Report, August 1993.
6. S. Contassot-Vivier, "Visualisation paralléle de MNT texturés", Master's thesis, Ecole Normale Supérieure de Lyon, June 1995.
7. F. C. Crow, G. Demos, J. Hardy, J. McLaughlin and K. Sims, "3D image synthesis on the connection machine", *Proc. Int. Conf. Parallel Processing for Computer Vision and Display*, Leeds, UK, January 1988.
8. D. A. Ellsworth, "A new algorithm for interactive graphics on multicomputers", *IEEE Computer*, July 1994, pp. 33–40.
9. E. Fiume, A. Fournier and L. Rudolph, "A parallel scan conversion algorithm with anti-aliasing for a general-purpose ultracomputer", *ACM Comput. Graphics* **17**, 3 (1983) 141–150.
10. M. Kaplan and D. P. Greenberg, "Parallel processing techniques for hidden surface removal", *Comput. Graphics, Proc. Siggraph* **13**, 2 (1979) 300–309.
11. S. Miguet and Y. Robert, "Elastic load balancing for image processing algorithms", in *Parallel Computation*, ed. H. P. Zima, Lecture Notes in Computer Science, Salzburg, Austria, September 1991, 1st International ACPC Conference, Springer-Verlag, pp. 438–451.
12. S. Molnar, M. Cox, D. Ellsworth and H. Fuchs, "A sorting classification of parallel rendering", *IEEE Comput. Graphics Appl.*, July 1994, pp. 23–32.
13. D. R. Roble, "A load balanced parallel scanline Z-buffer algorithm for the IPSC hypercube", *Proc. Pixel '88*, Paris, France, October 1988, Hermes.
14. D. S. Whelan, *Animac: A Multiprocessor Architecture for Real-Time Computer Animation*, PhD thesis, California Institute of Technology, 1985.
15. S. Whitman, "Dynamic load balancing for parallel polygon rendering," *IEEE Comput. Graphics Appl.* **14**, 4 (1994) 41–48.

 **Sylvain Contassot-Vivier** graduated from the Ecole Normale Supérieure de Lyon in 1995. He is currently a Ph.D. student in computer science at the LIP Laboratory of the ENS Lyon. He joined the image processing group of the ERIC Laboratory at the Lyon 2 University in 1997.

His main scientific interests lie in the design of parallel algorithms for image processing and computer graphics.

MODELING 3D DEFORMABLE OBJECT
WITH THE ACTIVE PYRAMID

PIERRE-JEAN REISSMAN and ISABELLE E. MAGNIN

CREATIS, INSA 502, 69621 Villeurbanne cedex, France
E-mail: isabelle.magnin@creatis.insa-lyon.fr

Medical imaging is a powerful mean to access dynamic function of 3D deformable organs of the body. Due to the flow of incoming data, multiresolution methods on parallel computers is the only way to achieve complex processings in reasonable time. We present an active pyramid to model dynamic volumes. This pyramid is built on the first volume of a sequence and contains a binary model of the objects of interest. Previous knowledge is introduced within this binary model. The structure of the pyramid is rigid, but its main interest is that its components are deformed to fit the data using energetical constraints. A multiresolution algorithm based on self-organizing maps is then applied to deform the model through time. This algorithm matches the different levels of the pyramid in a coarse to fine approach. The output of the matching process is the field of deformation, modeling the transformations. This pyramid is applied to real data in the result section. The rigid structure of the pyramid is suitable for massively parallel architectures.

Keywords: Pyramid, multiresolution, modeling, self-organization, matching.

1. INTRODUCTION

Recognition and modeling of 3D deformable and moving objects is one of the key issues in medical imaging. In this field, a huge flow of data is delivered by the various imaging devices such as X-Ray scanners, Magnetic Resonance and Ultrasonic imaging systems. Real time processing of the image sequences is often desirable and this is particularly true as far as cardiac imaging is concerned. Therefore, it comes out that parallel computing is today, the only reasonable way to envisage true 3D Cardiac Imaging.

Among the algorithms involved in both image processing and parallel computing, the pyramidal approaches are of great interest. Historically, the first pyramidal decompositions of an image, were based on a deterministic spatial partitioning of the image.[18,20] In order to improve the model, Meer[13] proposed to move from the previous rigid pyramidal model to a stochastic one. The use of such a model to segment images leads to unequal quality results, because the model remains independent of the image content. In 1990, Jolion, Montanvert and Rosenfeld[7,8,14] considered some local features of the image to influence the construction of the stochastic pyramid, leading to the adaptive pyramid. The improvement was good but not sufficient. As a matter of fact, the major drawback common to the rigid, stochastic and adaptive pyramidal techniques is their lack of adaptibility to the specificity of the image to be processed. Their main common advantage lies in their multiresolution aspect which provides both low-time computing and efficient

Parallel Image Analysis: Tools and Models (1998) 107–117

image processing. In 1993 Mathieu and Magnin proposed a new concept of soft pyramid,[11,12] able to adapt itself to the content of the image over the pyramidal decomposition. The principle consists, after the image-to-graph transform at *level 0*, to select a Minimal Spanning Tree (MST),[15] as the basis of the pyramid. The main advantage of the MST is its ability to follow and delineate the objects contained in the image. The structure of the soft pyramid is a continuous communication net linking the highly detailed pictures of the scene to the higher levels of representation. Modeling dynamic aspects of the objects is a second part of the study. The involved concepts are similar for both soft and rigid structures: given a model of an object at instant t what are the additive parameters to model the same object at time $t + 1$. A field of deformation is computed defining a homeomorphic transformation of the object contained in the picture (image or volume). The defined algorithm works both on rigid and soft pyramids. Recently Reissman and Magnin[17] proposed an active pyramid based on a regular mesh structure of given topology whose cells experience an adaptive geometry driven by the data. This active pyramid includes the dynamic aspect of the objects by a generic matching algorithm.

The paper takes place in this context. It is organized as follows: in Sec. 2, we briefly recall the main features of regular and irregular pyramids; in Sec. 3, we describe the Active pyramid. We address the problem of matching pyramids in Sec. 5. In Sec. 6 preliminary results of 2D and 3D deformable object modeling using the Active pyramids matching are presented.

2. THE PYRAMIDS

2.1. Classification

An image pyramid is a stack of images with regularly decreasing resolution. The bottom level, *level 0*, of a pyramid is the initial image. The simplest way to build a pyramid consists in low-pass filtering *level 0* and subsampling it afterwards to create *level 1*. Each level is recursively built that way until the top of the pyramid, level N, is reached. The structure of a pyramid is determined by the neighborhood relations within one level and the parent-children relations between adjacent levels. The structure of a pyramid can be represented by a set of graphs. Each level is a horizontal graph in which cells are connected by arcs. A vertical graph contains the cells of two adjacent levels connected by vertical links. The pyramidal structures can be classified in two classes: *regular* and *irregular*, see Fig. 1. Regular pyramids operate on a regular graph structure instead of the irregular neighborhoods as in the case of irregular pyramids.

Regular pyramids include Quadtrees[19,20] and Active pyramids.[17] They are based on a regular mesh with given topological properties. The regular graph structure is repeated throughout the pyramid in a multiscale frame. *Rigid regular pyramids* present a lack of adaptivity to the image content, as their only freedom degrees are the computed fields associated to each cell. This problem is overcome with active pyramids that use an elastic mesh (cf. Sec. 2). Regular pyramids are very simple to implement. They fit well on parallel architectures.

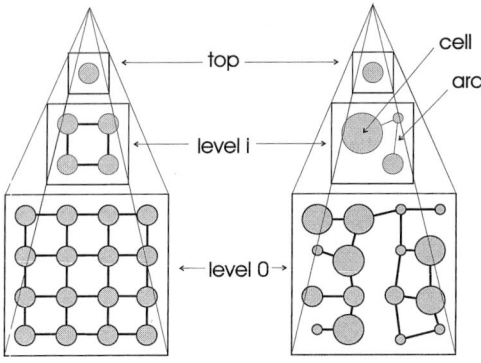

Fig. 1. Regular pyramid versus irregular (soft) pyramid.

Irregular pyramids[14] include Stochastic,[13] Adaptive,[7] Voronoi[2] and Soft[12] pyramids. They offer greater flexibility because they operate on a general graph structure instead of a regular graph structure. This graph (*level 1* of the pyramid) is an elementary adjacency graph for Stochastic and adaptive pyramids, a Delaunay graph for Voronoi pyramids and a Minimal Spanning Tree (MST) for Soft pyramids. The successive levels of irregular pyramids are built using a decimation process that selects the cells to remain in the upper level. The decimation process can be stochastic, adaptive or combined.

2.2. Structure

Several successive steps are involved in the bottom-up construction of an image pyramid. The image-to-graph transform is the initial step. It leads from the initial image I at *level 0* of the pyramid to a graph $G(C, A)$ at *level 1*, where C represents the set of cells of the current level and A the set of its arcs. At *level 1*, the pixels of I are the cells (or vertices) of $G(C, A)$. Two cells of the same level are connected by a valued arc. A recursive process allows to build *level L* from *level L_{-1}* until the top of the pyramid is reached. The vertical connections between the parent-cell of *level L* and the children-cells of *level L_{-1}* are called links. They are not valued. The specificity of the Active pyramid is detailed in the next section. Each step of the construction is described. The major particular features of this new class of pyramids are enhanced.

3. THE ACTIVE PYRAMID

3.1. An Elastic Mesh

The active pyramid is a regular pyramid. The graph $G(C, A)$ of *level 1* is the elementary adjacency graph. It is a regular mesh, where each cell is connected to its 4 nearest neighbors according to the chosen connectivity. But this mesh has a particular feature which makes it very attractive: it has elastic properties. Given input data and a "reference mesh", the problem is to deform the mesh so that it fits the data. In order to perform the fitting, we developed a technique based on deformable surfaces in which each node of the mesh is subjected to a force that is a function of the image content.

3.1.1. Nodal energy

*Image density energy

Let us note $G'(C', A')$ a dual graph of $G(C, A)$, as shown in Fig. 2. The "reference mesh" is a square grid superimposed to the image I'. I' is a filtered version of I (see (2)). Each node c' of $G'(C', A')$ lies on a point p' of the surface defined by I'. Each node c' is connected to its 4 neighbors by 4 arcs having elastic properties. A force $\vec{f_k}$ is pulling c' in the direction of its kth neighbors respectively. Its strength is proportional to the square of the distance computed on the geodesic path separating c' from each neighbor and calculated on the surface defined by I'. In other words, it depends on the local content of the enhanced image seen as a grey level mountain with enhanced relief at edges. At every node c', the resulting energy term is defined as a sum of the square modulus of the various forces. It is named E_d:

$$E_d = \left\| \sum_{k \in N(c')} \vec{f_k} \right\|^2 \tag{1}$$

where $N(c')$ is the neighborhood of c'. The term E_d closely depends on the local density properties of the image. For nodes c' located on the edges of G' the resulting force is projected on the vertical or/and horizontal axes as the neighborhood is not symmetric.

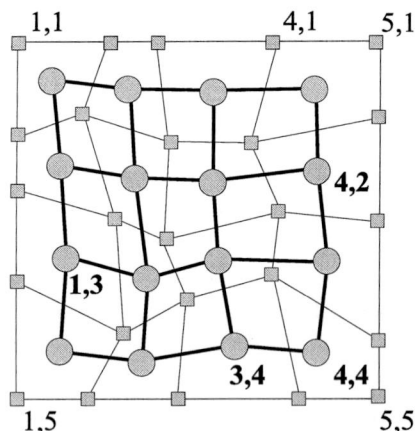

Fig. 2. Level L of the Active Pyramid with the elastic mesh. The two dual graphs $G(C, A)$ and $G'(C', A')$ are represented. The squares are the nodes c' of $G'(C', A')$. The circles are the cells c of $G(C, A)$. The region of interest of a cell c is the tetrahedron around it.

*Image gradient energy

The local gradient of the image is considered as a second term of the energy. It is used to enhance the edges of the picture defining I'. The minimization of the global energy E moves the nodes c' towards the closest extremum of gradient. The filtered version I' of I is defined as:

$$ I'(p) = \alpha_1 + \alpha_2 \cdot I(p) + \alpha_3 \cdot \left\| \frac{\nabla I(p)}{\max(\nabla I(p))} \right\|^{\beta} \quad \text{with} \quad 0 < \beta < 1, \qquad (2) $$

where $\alpha_1, \alpha_2, \alpha_3$ are real coefficients and the denominator holds for the maximum of gradient in the whole image. We note that the exponent β enhances the low-contrasted edges contained in the image, as its value tends to zero.

3.1.2. Global mesh energy

The total cost function E_M associated to the whole mesh is the contribution of all its nodes (3). It is given by:

$$ E_M = \sum_{c' \in C'} E_d(c') \qquad (3) $$

where C' is the set of nodes of the graph $G'(C', A')$ at one level of the pyramid.

3.1.3. Generating the mesh

The mesh is built iteratively. At iteration t, the global mesh energy E_M is calculated from the sum of the energy terms $E(c')$ related to each node. Then the nodes move locally to decrease their local energy. The solution is reached when the decrease of E_M becomes inefficient.

During the minimization process, three constraints must be satisfied to keep to the fundamental properties of the mesh:

- Its topology has to be maintained: no overlapping between cells allowed,
- It has local adaptivity: the region of interest of a cell is spatially limited,
- It must cover the whole image: border nodes are not allowed to collapse towards the center of the image.

3.2. A Classical Construction

The Active pyramid is a regular pyramid. Each *level L* is a low-pass filtered version of *level L_{-1}* followed by a subsampling by two in each direction. At each level, an elastic mesh is iteratively fitted to the image contents as just described.

3.3. Modeling Information

At each level of the pyramid, a graph $G(C, A)$ is defined as the dual of $G'(C', A')$. Each cell c of $G(C, A)$ represents a region of interest (ROI) of the image, that is an elastic tetrahedon $T(c)$ limited by 4 adjacent nodes c' of $G'(C', A')$. A features vector $V(c)$ is extracted from each ROI and attached to its representative cell. The retained features are heterogeneous in nature, they model information related to the processed image. We have selected 7 features: *the 1st and 2nd statistical moments* of the cell c (i.e. calculated on $T(c)$), *the 1st and 2nd statistical moments* of its neighborhood $N(c)$, *the entropy* of c and *its coordinates* (i, j) in the image plane, *a label* corresponding to prior knowledge concerning the cell.

3.4. Conclusion

Active pyramids use a regular mesh whose geometrical aspect is largely influenced by the local image content. The topology is conserved throughout the multiscale frame but the shape of the cells may significantly vary. Those are elastic tetrahedrons whose sides differ in length according to the local image density and gradients. They deform and move so as to minimize some energy function related to the image content. The active pyramid overall structure is specially well adapted for parallel computing, because each cell has a constant number of neighbors.

4. NEURAL PYRAMID MATCHING

We now address the matching problem between two successive images of a sequence: given two pyramidal models associated to each image respectively, determine the elastic transform between the 2 instances of the data. The most straightforward approach is to compute a distance measure between the pyramids which is minimum for the best transform. We define a coarse-to-fine strategy that consists in matching the cells of the two pyramids level after level, from the apex to the base, see Fig. 3.

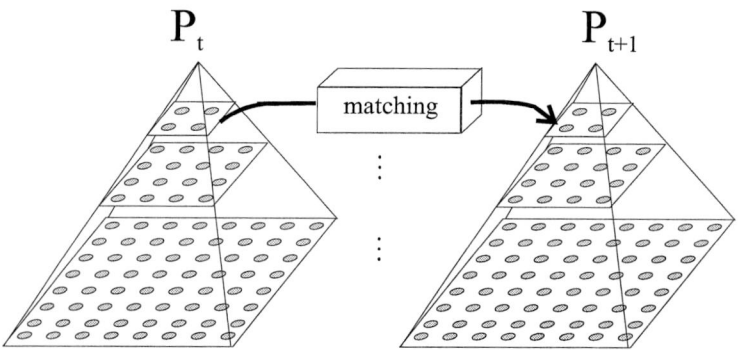

Fig. 3.   Coarse-to-fine strategy using a recursive matching between two active pyramids.

4.1. Multiscale Self-Organizing Maps

The active pyramid is a set of N graphs, one of them for each level from the apex to the base. We note that a graph can be seen as a self-organizing map, or network, as its structure is similar. Indeed, it contains cells c with their associated features vector $V(c)$. The cells divide the representation space into elementary regions. The size of the input space related to every network equals the dimension of the features vector.

4.1.1. Definition of a distance

The problem is now to find the best match between two active pyramids P_t and P_{t+1}. This is done by defining a distance between the graphs $G(C, A)_t$ and $G(C, A)_{t+1}$ as the min difference between the feature vectors of cells c_t and c_{t+1} respectively. Formally, the distance between two cells of *level L* is defined as:

$$d_L(c_t, c_{t+1}) = \sum_{k \in V(c)} \sqrt{\eta_k (V_{k,t} - V_{k,t+1})^2} \qquad (4)$$

where $V_{k,t}$, and $V_{k,t+1}$, represent the components of the feature vector attached to every cell of the corresponding levels in the pyramids P_t and P_{t+1} respectively. The parameter η_k is a normalization parameter attached to each component of the feature vector. The problem is now to minimize, following a coherent strategy. The best matching leading to the elastic transform T at *level L* is obtained when the sum of the minimum elementary distances (6) between all the corresponding cells of P_t and P_{t+1} at *level L* is minimum. It can be written:

$$d_L^*(c_t, c_{t+1}) = \sum_{C_L} \|d_{min}(c_t, c_{t+1})\|^2 \qquad (5)$$

where C_L is the set of cells at *level L*.

4.2. Minimization Process

The proposed iterative process consists of minimizing d_L for the N levels of pyramids sequentially. The minimization results in defining a geometrical translation vector for each cell c. We use a coarse-to-fine strategy to match the two active pyramids. The process is divided in three steps, applied to each *level L* of the pyramids.

4.2.1. Computing the inter-cells distances

The first step consists for every cell c of G_t (in *level L* of P_t) to compute the distance that separates it from all the corresponding cells of G_{t+1} located in a geometrical neighborhood whose size decreases linearly versus the iterations as shown in Fig. 4. Moreover the influence of a cell of P_{t+1} decreases as the Euclidean distance with c increases. The cell of G_{t+1}, closest to c in the sense that it minimizes the distance, is selected. But it is available to note that, in practice, the correspondence between cells is not a bijection and a same cell of G_{t+1} can be selected several times, as the closest one, by different cells of G_t. This phenomenon is particularly enhanced in the areas of the image with homogeneous density. To solve the conflict, a penality factor s is introduced. It artificially increases the distance between a cell of G_t and one of G_{t+1} proportionally to the previous selections. The new definitions of d is therefore:

$$d(c_t, c_{t+1}) = d(c_t, c_{t+1}) + s. \qquad (6)$$

After one iteration, every cell of G_t has a matched cell in G_{t+1}.

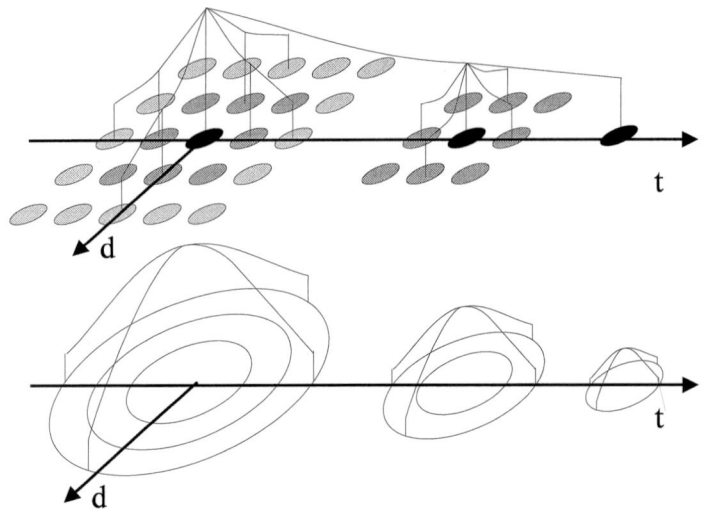

Fig. 4. Upper: Active neighborhood of a cell decreasing versus iterations t. Lower: weighting function decreasing the influence of the neighboring cells with the Euclidean distance.

4.2.2. Elastic motion of the cells

Once the matched cell has been found, the cell c of G_t moves, with its neighborhood, towards the geometrical position of its correspondent in G_{t+1}. The translation is weighted to preserve a regular structure to the graph. In other words, the translation remains always less than the Euclidean distance separating the two cells, so that no overlapping occurs. When all the cells have modified their position, they are recentered within their neighborhood as shown in Fig. 5.

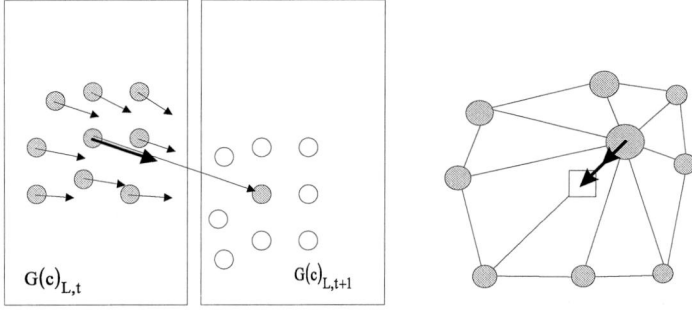

Fig. 5. Left: Levels L of pyramids G_t and G_{t+1}. The cell c of G_t and its active neighborhood are translated towards the matched cell of G_{t+1}. Right: Graph shaping: the matched cells are recentered within their neighborhood.

4.2.3. Iterative process

It is an iterative process and the selection and adaption steps are repeated until the process converges towards a solution.

The solution obtained at *level L* is then propagated to *level L_{-1}* where it is considered as the initial solution for this level. The iterative process is then applied at *level L_{-1}* and so on to the base.

5. RESULTS

We have applied the active pyramid model to 2D sequences of MRI images of a moving heart. The elastic mesh is of great interest in this context, because the heart is a deformable muscle producing a complex motion and deformation. An example of two images with their corresponding pyramids is shown in Fig. 6. We can easily observe the local deformation of the mesh, at the various scales, due to the local heart deformation. The concept of the Active pyramid has been extended in 3D. It has been applied to model a temporal sequence of 3D X-ray angiography of a dog's left ventricle (LV). Figure 7 shows an example of two 3D volumes of the left ventricle at telesystolic and telediastolic phases of the cycle.

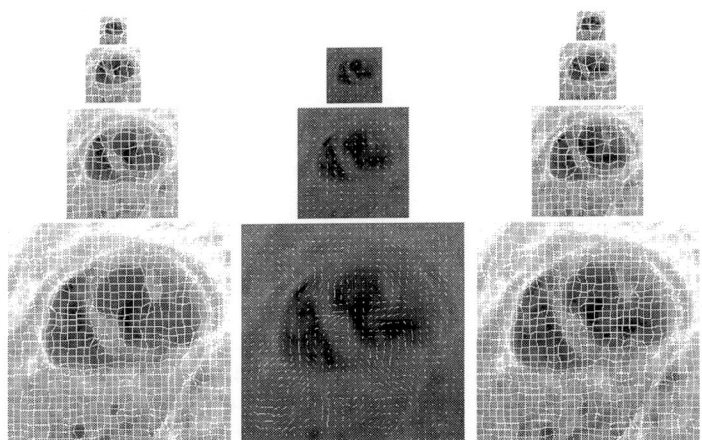

Fig. 6. Times 10 and 11 of a temporal sequence of MRI short axis views of a beating heart. The pyramid in between, shows the vector field of deformation between the two images.

6. CONCLUSION

We proposed a new concept of Active pyramid associated to a general coarse-to-fine matching strategy for pyramids. The main interest of this model is that it can easily handle various image features and prior knowledge in an elastic multiscale framework. The pyramid matching process allows to model local elastic deformation and motion, at different scales, from a sequence of 2D or 3D data.

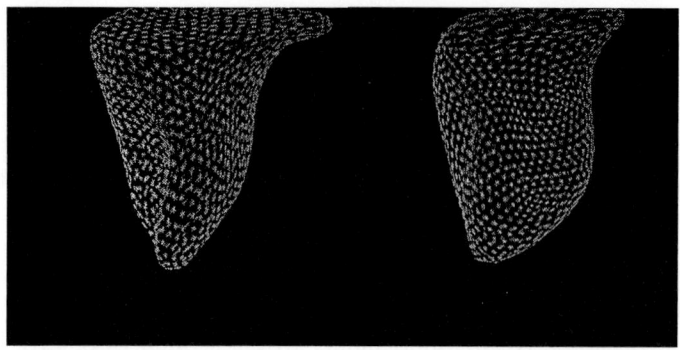

Fig. 7. Two 3D endocardial walls, at a given resolution level, with a display of the cells provided by an isotropic elastic and spherical mesh fitted to the data.

7. ACKNOWLEDGMENTS

This work is part of the project entitled "Nouvelles architectures parallèles et développement d'applications" supported by a grant of the Région Rhone-Alpes. The topic is related to the GDR ISIS of the CNRS. The authors thank Professors Robb and Rittman, at the Mayo Clinic, for providing the data.

REFERENCES

1. R. S. Barr, R. V. Helgaon and J. L. Kennington, "Minimal spanning trees: an empirical investigation of parallel algorithms", *Parall. Comput.* **12**, 1 (1989) 45–52.
2. E. Bertin, H. Bischof and P. Bertolino, "Voronoi pyramids controlled by Hopfield neural networks", *CVGIP*, 1994.
3. P. Clermont, "Contrôle et programmation des réseaux pyramidaux", in *Algorithmique Parallèle*, Masson, Paris, 1992.
4. J. L. Crawley and A. C. Sanderson, "Multiple resolution representation and probabilistic matching of 2-D gray scale shape", *IEEE Trans. Patt. Anal. Mach. Intell.* **9**, 1 (1987) 13–121.
5. M. Hebert, K. Ikeuchi and H. Delingette, "A spherical representation for recognition of free-form surfaces", *IEEE Trans. Patt. Anal. Mach. Intell.* **17**, 7 (1995) 681–690.
6. W. C. Huang and D. B. Goldgof, "Adaptive-size meshes for rigid and nonrigid shape analysis and synthesis", *IEEE Trans. Patt. Anal. Mach. Intell.* **15**, 6 (1993) 611–616.
7. J. M. Jolion and A. Montanvert, "The adaptive pyramid: a framework for 2D image analysis", *Comput. Vision Graphics Image Process.: Image Understanding* **55**, 3 (1992) 339–348.
8. J.-M. Jolion and A. Rosenfeld, "A pyramid framework for early vision", Kluwer Academic Publishers, Dordrecht, Boston, London, 1994.
9. T. Kohonen, *Self Organization and Associative Memory*, Springer-Verlag, Berlin, 1984.
10. J. B. Kruskal, Jr., "On the shortest subtree of a graph and the traveling salesman problem", *Proc. Am. Math. Soc.* **7** (1956) 48–50.
11. C. Mathieu, "Segmentation d'images par pyramides souples: application à l'imagerie médicale multidimensionnelle", Ph.D. thesis: Institut National des Sciences appliquées, France, 1993, pp. 228.
12. C. Mathieu and I. E. Magnin, "On the choice of the first level of graph pyramids", *J. Math. Image Vision* **6** (1996) 85–89.

COMPLEXITY ANALYSIS OF A PARALLEL IMPLEMENTATION OF THE MARCHING-CUBES ALGORITHM

SERGE MIGUET*

Laboratoire ERIC, bâtiment L, Université Lumière Lyon 2
5, avenue Pierre Mendes, 69676 Bron Cedex, France
E-mail: Serge.Miguet@univ-lyon2.fr

JEAN-MARC NICOD*

Laboratoire d'Informatique de Besançon, IUT Belfort Montbéliard
BP 527 Rue Engel Gros, 90016 Belfort, France
E-mail: Jean-Marc.Nicod@iut-bm.univ-fcomte.fr

This paper presents a load-balanced parallelization of the well known Marching-Cubes algorithm, that aims at constructing an iso-surface in a 3D image. We first derive a modelization for the computation time as a function of the generated surface complexity. The workload associated to each slice of the input data is evaluated by counting the number of vertices that will be generated on that slice. The slices are then locally redistributed to ensure a balanced workload. We give an upper bound on the number of polygons of the triangulation, and present a family of surfaces whose number of triangles tends to this bound. This analysis allows us to foresee (and thus to allocate) the memory size needed for the data structures and to assign to each vertex a unique global reference.

Experiments done on an Intel Paragon machine are given both for synthetic and medical images. They show the usefulness of our dynamic data redistribution scheme.

Keywords: Marching-cubes, dynamic load balancing, parallel computing, medical imaging, surface extraction.

1. INTRODUCTION

With the popularization of 3D scanning devices and acquisition modalities used for medical applications, many new algorithms have been developed for the reconstruction, processing and visualization of 3D images. There are essentially two main ways for computing a 2D view of the objects present in a 3D volume: direct visualization algorithms, and techniques based on the extraction of the surfaces of the objects, chained with classical surface rendering algorithms.

In the direct visualization techniques, no segmentation of the objects is necessary: each voxel of the 3D volume is assigned a color and an opacity value, and might influence the final image when it is projected to the screen. There are several ways to compute this projection. The most popular algorithms are based on ray-casting: a ray is cast from the eye of the observer through each pixel of the screen. The intersected voxels accumulate their colors along the view ray depending on their respective opacity. These techniques allow to produce pictures with a great degree of realism, and permit to see simultaneously several kind of objects

---

*Authors were members of the LIP Laboratory of the Ecole Normale Supérieure de Lyon when this work was completed.

Parallel Image Analysis: Tools and Models (1998) 119–131
© World Scientific Publishing Company

(tumor, bones, skin) by the use of different colors and level of transparency. On the other hand, they are very compute intensive since the whole volume data has to be scanned for each different position of the observer.

The other visualization techniques begin by a segmentation step, where the surfaces of interest are extracted from the volume data. We lose the possibility to see simultaneously different surfaces, but many images can be computed for different points of view without having to re-scan the whole volume. Several approaches can be used to produce these surfaces: The oldest algorithms compute 1D contours on each slice of the volume, and then construct a triangulation between corresponding contours. The main problem is to solve the ambiguity when branching structures make one contour divide into several ones on the neighboring slice. A more robust technique called the *Marching-Cubes* algorithm was proposed by Lorensen and Cline in 1987.[4] It is a true 3D segmentation technique that computes a triangulated surface corresponding to an iso-density value. The surface separates the voxels whose values are on both sides of the chosen threshold. The surface produced by this algorithm is very accurate and can render small details of the objects, since the size of the generated surface elements are of the same order of magnitude as the sampling period.

One of the objectives of our research group is to design an efficient environment for 3D image processing. The interactive choice of the threshold value in the Marching-Cubes algorithm would be a very interesting feature for the computer-assisted detection of particular internal structures. The whole surface has to be recomputed quickly for each threshold value, thus requiring a very important computational power. Together with the fact that very large data sets have to be manipulated makes natural the use of massively parallel implementation of these algorithms.

The goal of this paper is to present an efficient parallel implementation of the Marching-Cubes algorithm on a distributed memory machine. Section 2 first presents the sequential algorithm as introduced in Ref. 4. Some details are given on the non-redundant data structure we use to represent the surface. An important point introduced in this paper that improves our first results presented in Ref. 6 concerns memory management. Indeed, we show how to efficiently foresee the size of the data structures needed to represent the surface.

Section 3 describes then our parallel implementation whose basic principle is to equally distribute the volume data to the processors. Two main issues are discussed in this section. Firstly, the surface computed in parallel should be the same as the one obtained by the sequential algorithm. This point is complicated by the non-redundancy of our surface representation, but can be solved by local communications only. Secondly, we point out that the initial idea to equally partition the volume data is not always efficient when the surface of interest is not uniformly distributed. Indeed, our experimental results show that the computation time is much higher in those regions of the space where surface elements are generated. According to a workload estimation, we propose to redistribute locally the volume data to reach a balanced computation time among the processors.

Section 4 finally presents experimental results obtained on both medical and artificial images. We compare the sequential execution time to the parallel time measured on an Intel Paragon machine. We also illustrate the usefulness of our dynamic data redistribution for balancing the load of the processors.

2. THE MARCHING-CUBES ALGORITHM

2.1. Computation of the Surface

Let us assume that our input data is a discrete 3D image, mapping a value $V(x, y, z)$ to each point (x, y, z) of $\mathcal{Z}^3$ with $0 \leq x \leq X$, $0 \leq y \leq Y$ and $0 \leq z \leq Z$. $V(x, y, z)$ is called the density of this point. The set of points such that $x = 0$, $x = X$, $y = 0$, $y = Y$, $z = 0$, $z = Z$ is called the border of the image. We will assume in the following that $V(x, y, z) = 0$ for any border point.

As mentioned in the introduction, the goal of the Marching-Cubes algorithm is to construct a surface corresponding to an iso-density value. This is done by considering cubic cells of coordinates (x, y, z) whose vertices are placed on the 8 input samples $(x + i, y + j, z + k)$ of the volume data, with $i, j, k \in \{0, 1\}$. The algorithm computes the way the surface intersects a given cell, generates triangles for this cell, and then moves to the next cell (the cube "marches").

The iso-surface has an intersection with a cell if some of the values of the 8 input samples are below the iso-surface level, while others are above. The topology of the triangulation associated to a cell only depends on whether vertices are above or below the iso-surface level: for instance, if all vertices have a value below or above the threshold, there is no intersection, and thus no generated triangles. Since we have only two possibilities for each vertex, we deduce that there are 256 possible configurations for the intersection. A possible way to encode the configurations is to assign one bit per vertex, set to 1 if and only if the corresponding sample is "inside" the surface. We can thus compute a 8 bits index for each configuration. This index gives access to one out of 256 entries of a configuration table, describing the topology associated to this configuration.

The authors show that due to symmetries and rotations, we only have to record for the 14 different topologies represented in Fig. 1. Several authors propose slight modifications of this analysis, showing that some of the standard cases (case number 10 for instance) are ambiguous.[5,8] We won't focus here on this, since we are mostly interested in the parallelization topic.

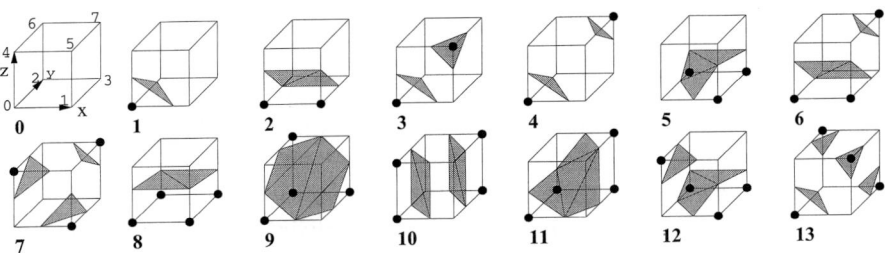

Fig. 1. The 14 different standard triangulations.

When looking at Fig. 1, we see that the vertices of the triangulation are always located on the edges of the cell. A simple solution would be to place them in the middle of the edge, but Lorensen and Cline propose an intuitively better solution: they use the iso-density value together with the two samples located at the extremities of the edge, and then perform a linear interpolation to place the vertex. More precisely, let V_1 and V_2 be the samples of the extremities of an edge, and V be the intersection of the surface with that edge. The position of V on the edge is such that:

$$\frac{\overline{V_1V}}{\overline{V_1V_2}} = \frac{v - v_1}{v_2 - v_1}$$

where v_1 and v_2 are the values of V_1 and V_2 respectively, and v is the iso-surface level. Note that no vertex is generated on that edge if v is not between v_1 and v_2.

For the purpose of shaded visualization of the surface, it is useful to know the normal to the surface on each vertex of the triangulation. The choice in Ref. 4 was to linearly interpolate the centered gradient in V_1 and V_2, to have an approximation of the normal in V.

In Fig. 2, we illustrate the surface generated by the algorithm. Our input image is the torus of Fig. 2(a). Background voxels have value 0 while foreground voxels have value 2. In Fig. 2(b), we used the iso-surface level of 2, resulting to vertices stick to the surface of the torus. In Fig. 2(c), the iso-surface level is chosen to value 1, giving the impression of "inflating" the object. Figure 2(d) is a surface rendering with Gouraud shading of the same surface.

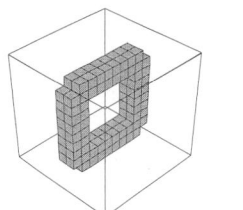 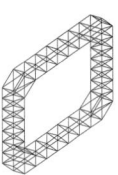 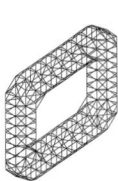 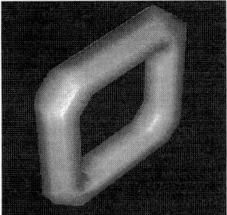

Fig. 2. Result of the algorithm on a synthetic example.

2.2. Non-Redundant Representation of the Surface

As mentioned above, the algorithm generates the triangulation for a single cell, and then moves to the next cell according to a predefined scanning order (e.g. the increasing z, y and x axis). When arriving at a new cell, the algorithm does not have to compute all the vertices associated to the current triangulation, since some of them might have been computed for already scanned neighboring cells. Using this remark, we can assure that each vertex is computed only once.

A naive way to represent the surface would be to generate a set of triangles, each composed of 3 vertices. One vertex would be represented by its 3 space coordinates and the 3 coordinates of its normal. Nevertheless, this representation is space consuming since the number of triangles to which a given vertex can belong is between 4 and 12. Moreover, if we assume that the surface computation is chained to a surface visualization, the projection of each vertex would be recomputed the same number of times.

For these reasons, we have chosen a two-level representation scheme, where vertices are stored once and only once, and are associated to a unique index (vertices are numbered from 0 to $\mathcal{V}-1$ where $\mathcal{V}$ is the total number of vertices). Each triangle is then simply represented by three vertex indices.

2.3. Memory Management

The Marching-Cubes algorithm is a very memory consuming application. The input 3D image typically represents 25 Megabytes of storage (100 slices of 512×512 resolution). The number of generated triangles is then of the order of one million, with 12 bytes per triangles and about half as much vertices with 24 bytes per vertex. It results in about 50 Megabytes storage. Systems having not enough main memory can compute the surface "on the fly", while loading only a few slices of the input data, computing the partial surface and storing it before loading the next slices.

Since we are motivated by an interactive system, we have to keep all the data in main memory, which makes distributed memory systems even more attractive, independently of their computational power. In this framework, it is thus very important to minimize the size associated to the generated triangulation. Two solutions could be used: the first one would be to allocate memory step by step, while generating the surface, which implies the management of a pointer based data structure and the use of often costly memory allocation functions. For these reasons, we prefer the second solution consisting of first scanning the data to estimate the size of the surface, then allocating the memory we will need for both the vertices and the triangles. Furthermore, as we will see in Sec. 3.2, the number of vertices will be useful for the purpose of workload estimation.

Determining the number of vertices $\mathcal{V}$ of the triangulation is very easy: for each edge cell, i.e. for each pair of adjacent samples of respective values v_1 and v_2, a vertex will be generated on that edge if and only if the iso-surface level v is between v_1 and v_2. We explain in the discussion (see Sec. 5.2) how this step can be greatly improved in the case of multiple surface extractions.

Determining exactly the number of triangles $\mathcal{T}$ is not as easy. We prefer using an upper bound for $\mathcal{T}$ that can be derived from $\mathcal{V}$ with a simple formula $\mathcal{T} \leq \gamma \mathcal{V}$. In the following we derive the best possible value of γ. Before expressing the theorem which gives this optimal bound let us formulate the following definitions:

- Let C be the set of all cells of the image, and c an element of C.
- Let v be a vertex of the iso-surface.
- Let $\mathcal{V}(c)$ be the number of vertices of the triangulation in the cell c.
- Let $\mathcal{T}_c(v)$ be the number of triangles incident to the vertex v in the cell c.
- Let $\mathcal{T}(v)$ be the total number of triangles incident to the vertex v.

Lemma 1. The average number of $\mathcal{T}_c(v)$ in a given cell c is bounded by 2. In other

13. P. Meer, "Stochastic image pyramids", *Comput. Vision, Graphics Image Process.* **45** (1989) 269–294.

14. A. Montanvert, P. Meer and A. Rosenfeld, "Hierarchical image analysis using irregular tesselations", *IEEE Trans. Patt. Anal. Mach. Intell.* **13**, 4 (1991) 307–316.

15. O. J. Morris, M. J. Lee and A. G. Constantinides, "Graph theory for image analysis: an approach based on the shortest spanning tree", *IEEE Proc. F. Commun. Radar Signal Process.* **133** (1986) 146–152.

16. R. C. Prim, "Shortest connection networks", *The Bell Syst. Tech. J.* **36** (1957) 1389–1401.

17. P. J. Reissman, P. Clarysse and I. E. Magnin, "Modélisation et mise en correspondance avec la pyramide neuractive", *Traitement du Signal* **13**, 6 (1997) in press.

18. A. Rosenfeld, *Multiresolution Image Processing and Analysis*, Springer-Verlag, Berlin, 1984.

19. H. Samet, *The Design and Analysis of Spatial Data Structures*, Addison Wesley, 1990.

20. S. Tanimoto and T. Pavlidis, "A hierarchical data structure for picture processing", *Comput. Graphics Image Process.* **4**, 2 (1975) 104–119.

21. Y. Wang and O. Lee, "Active mesh — A feature seeking and tracking image sequence representation scheme", *IEEE Trans. Image Process.* **3**, 5 (1994) 610–624.

Pierre-Jean Reissman received the Diploma of Engineer (electrical engineering) from the National Institute for Applied Sciences of Lyon in 1993. He is a Ph.D student since 1993 at CREATIS. The topic of his Ph.D thesis is to model dynamic 3D objects with pyramidal approaches.

Isabelle E. Magnin received the Diploma of Engineer from the Ecole Catholique des Arts et Métiers (ECAM) of Lyon, France, the Doctor engineering degree (1981) and the "Doctorat ès Sciences" (1987), from the National Institute for Applied Sciences (INSA) of Lyon. Since 1982 she has been a researcher with the National Institute for Health and Medical Research (INSERM) in Lyon, France.

Her main interest concerns 2D and 3D medical imaging. She is a member of the IEEE.

words, the following formula holds:

$$\frac{\sum_{v \in c} \mathcal{T}_c(v)}{\mathcal{V}(c)} \leq 2$$

Proof. The cell c is generated by one of the 14 standard triangulations (see Fig. 1). For all these triangulations, the number of triangles sharing a same vertex is equal to 1, 2 or 3. But we note that each time we have a vertex shared by three triangles, we can associate to this vertex another vertex belonging to only one triangle. We deduce from this remark that in a cell, the number of triangles incident to a same vertex is in average less than or equal to 2.   □

Lemma 2.

$$\sum_{c \in C} \mathcal{V}(c) = 4\mathcal{V}$$

Proof. Each vertex belongs to an edge of a cell (see Fig. 1). Each edge is shared by four different cells. Therefore each vertex is counted four times in the summation. Thus the sum of all vertices in all cells is equal to four times the number of vertices $\mathcal{V}$ of the triangulation.   □

We are now ready to announce the main theorem for the memory management:

Theorem. The number of triangles which are computed with the Marching-Cubes algorithm admits an upper bound which is a linear function of the number of vertices as expressed in the following formula:

$$\mathcal{T} \leq \gamma \mathcal{V}$$

where the smallest possible constant value for γ is $\frac{8}{3}$. In other words, the $\frac{\mathcal{T}}{\mathcal{V}}$ ratio is always smaller than $\frac{8}{3}$, but for any $\varepsilon > 0$, we can find a 3D image for which the triangulation admits a $\frac{\mathcal{T}}{\mathcal{V}}$ ratio larger than $(\frac{8}{3} - \varepsilon)$.

Proof. For any vertex v, $\mathcal{T}(v)$ can be decomposed as the following expression:

$$\mathcal{T}(v) = \mathcal{T}_{c_1}(v) + \mathcal{T}_{c_2}(v) + \mathcal{T}_{c_3}(v) + \mathcal{T}_{c_4}(v)$$

where c_i are the four cells incident to v (see Fig. 3).

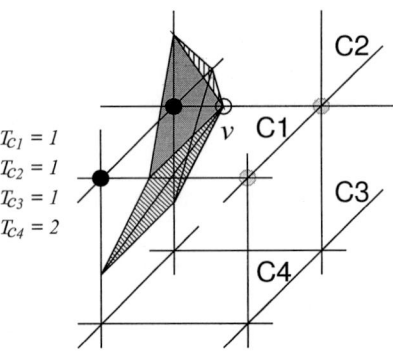

Fig. 3. Number of triangles incident to a vertex s for the four cells sharing the edge of v.

Let M be the average number of triangles incident to one vertex for all the vertices of the triangulation. We have:

$$M = \frac{1}{\mathcal{V}} \sum_{v} \mathcal{T}(v) \tag{1}$$

$$= \frac{1}{\mathcal{V}} \sum_{v} \sum_{i=1}^{4} \mathcal{T}_{c_i}(v) . \tag{2}$$

By changing the order of the terms in the sum (2), we get:

$$M = \frac{1}{\mathcal{V}} \sum_{c \in C} \sum_{v \in c} \mathcal{T}_c(v) . \tag{3}$$

From Lemma 1 we have:

$$\sum_{v \in c} \mathcal{T}_c(v) \leq 2\mathcal{V}(c) . \tag{4}$$

If we substitute (4) in (3), we obtain:

$$M \leq \frac{1}{\mathcal{V}} \sum_{c \in C} 2\mathcal{V}(c) . \tag{5}$$

Hence,

$$M \leq \frac{2}{\mathcal{V}} \sum_{c \in C} \mathcal{V}(c) . \tag{6}$$

Thus, from Lemma 2, we obtain that:

$$M \leq 8 . \tag{7}$$

In the expression of M (see Eq. (1)), each triangle is counted three times:

$$\sum_{v} \mathcal{T}(v) = 3\mathcal{T} . \tag{8}$$

Therefore,

$$M = 3\frac{\mathcal{T}}{\mathcal{V}} . \tag{9}$$

From Eqs. (7) and (9) we finally obtain:

$$\mathcal{T} \leq \frac{8}{3}\mathcal{V} . \tag{10}$$

$\square$

The value of $\frac{8}{3}$ is the best possible value of γ as was previously stated. Even if the $\frac{\mathcal{T}}{\mathcal{V}}$ ratio is often close to 2, we can build a family of surfaces for which the ratio tends to $\frac{8}{3}$.

For example, let V be a 3D image of dimension $n \times n \times n$ defined as follows:

$$V(i, j, k) = \begin{cases} 0 & \text{if } (i, j, k) \text{ is a voxel of the border, or 2 or 3 coordinates among} \\ & i, j, k \text{ are odd.} \\ 2 & \text{elsewhere.} \end{cases}$$

And let us consider a threshold value of 1.

We define border cells B as those cells having at least one of their vertices on the border of the image. The inner cells are then defined as $I = C \setminus B$.

It is easy to check that the configurations of the inner cells are generated by the standard configuration number 9 (see Fig. 1). Only the cells border might present a different configuration.

In this case the expression of M given by Eq. (3) can be rewritten as follows:

$$
M = \frac{1}{\mathcal{V}} \left(\sum_{c \in I} \sum_{v \in c} \mathcal{T}_c(v) + \sum_{c \in B} \sum_{v \in c} \mathcal{T}_c(v) \right)
$$

$$
= \frac{8 \times \mathcal{V}_{inner}}{\mathcal{V}} + \frac{\beta \times \mathcal{V}_{border}}{\mathcal{V}}.
$$

where $\beta \leq 8$.

Therefore, since $\mathcal{V}_{inner} = O(n^3)$, $\mathcal{V} = O(n^3)$ and $\mathcal{V}_{border} = O(n^2)$ we have:

$$
\lim_{n \to \infty} M = 8.
$$

From Eq. (9) we obtain:

$$
\lim_{n \to \infty} \frac{\mathcal{T}}{\mathcal{V}} = \frac{8}{3}.
$$

3. PARALLEL IMPLEMENTATION

In this section, we explain the main problems associated to the parallel implementation of the Marching-Cubes algorithm. Some authors have already proposed parallel versions of the algorithm, both for SIMD and MIMD machines. All these implementations use the intrinsic parallel nature of the algorithm, and divide the volume into contiguous blocks of data. Indeed, each cell can be considered independently from the others, if we accept some kind of redundancy in the computations.

3.1. Related Works

In Ref. 5, Mackerras proposes an implementation for the Fujitsu AP1000, a MIMD distributed memory machine with up to 128 processors. Each processor computes independent parts of the triangulation, for all the cells it is responsible for. The obtained surface is thus redundant, since the vertices that are common to neighboring processors are computed several times. The more processors in the machine, the more redundant the surface. Mackerras claims that communicating the vertices would be more expensive than duplicating the computations. We discuss this point later. As explained in Sec. 2.2, the rendering step is also penalized by the surface redundancy. Furthermore, Mackerras uses a static allocation of the data, that can lead to load imbalances as illustrated in Sec. 3.2.

In Ref. 9, Zheng and Nguyen use a SIMD machine, the Wavetracer Zephyr to parallelize the algorithm. Their implementation uses the same two-level data structure as the one exposed in Sec. 2.1, leading to a non-redundant surface. Their algorithm is an improvement of the algorithm of Ref. 3 initially designed for the CM-2. In the latter, after a complete data-parallel computation of configuration indexes, and generation of the vertices, the sequencer loops sequentially through the 256 different indexes, and the (virtual) processing elements concerned by the current index generate the triangles. The improvement proposed by Zheng and Nguyen consists in factorizing some of the 256 cases, and reducing the number of really different cases to 63. Since our target machines are asynchronous, we don't have to care about performing the same operation on different processors, which was crucial for synchronous parallel computers.

To our knowledge, no previous studies have taken into account the load-balancing problem. We show in the next section that this issue can be very important, and explain how to handle it.

3.2. The New Load-Balanced and Non-Redundant Algorithm

In order to illustrate the fact that the computing time of the Marching-Cubes algorithm is strongly data-dependent, we plot in Fig. 4 the execution time of the algorithm as a function of the number of vertices in the surface, for various image resolutions. To do this, we start from a random 3D image, and let the iso-density level vary, raising surfaces with highly variable number of vertices. The curves of Fig. 4 are straight lines, confirming that the execution time is the sum of a constant term, proportional to the number of visited cells, plus a time proportional to the number of generated vertices. More precisely, we have the following estimation for the execution time:

$$T(\mathcal{N}, \mathcal{V}) = \alpha \mathcal{N} + \beta \mathcal{V} \tag{11}$$

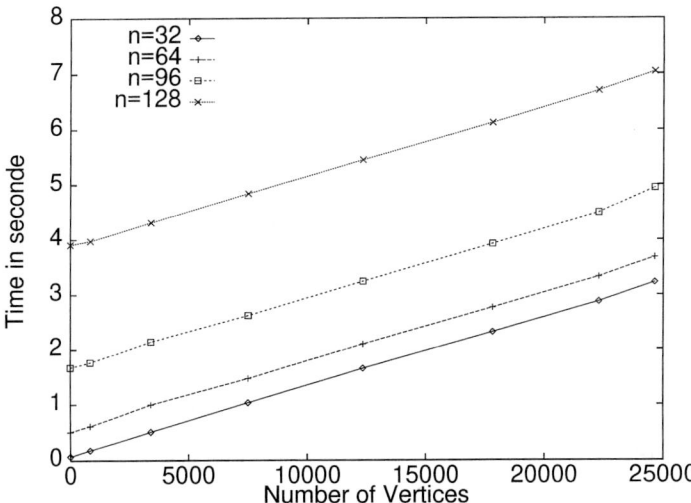

Fig. 4. Execution time as a function of the number of vertices in the surface of an image $n \times n \times n$.

where $\mathcal{N}$ is the number of scanned cells, $\mathcal{V}$ is the number of generated vertices, α is the time to compute the configuration index plus some control and β is the time to compute the real position and normal of a vertex of the triangulation. A simple linear regression gives the following numerical parameters, measured for the paragon machine:

$$\alpha = 1.99\mu\text{-seconds per cell}$$
$$\beta = 128\mu\text{-seconds per vertex}$$

When using static data allocation functions, some of the processors might have much more surface elements to generate than the others, and thus would penalize the global performance of the application. By using dynamic allocation strategies based on the elastic load-balancing algorithm,[2,7] we can allocate data so as to reach a balanced workload. This redistribution algorithm supposes that the data are mapped to a linear network of processors. We use thus allocations based upon contiguous slices of data (e.g. perpendicular to the z axis). Slices are then transmitted between adjacent processors so that each sub-domain has an approximately equivalent workload. The redistribution algorithm needs an estimation of the workload associated to each slice. According to Eq. (11), all what we need to do this estimation is to know the number of vertices that will be generated on each slice.

As explained in Sec. 2.3, this work has already been done for the purpose of memory use determination. A simple application of Eq. (11) to each slice allows to estimate the workload of each slice.

After the redistribution of the slices has been done, each processor is responsible for a certain (variable) number of slices. Let us give some more details about how the data are referenced: Suppose we dispose of a p processors machine, with individual processors numbered from 0 to $p-1$. Assume that the input data consists of $Z+1$ horizontal slices numbered from 0 to Z. The two consecutive slices z and $z+1$ form what we call the z *layer*. There are thus Z layers numbered from 0 to $Z-1$. In the redistribution step, the load is in fact associated to the layers, and individual processors are responsible for the computation of independent layers: Processor q is allocated layers of indices l such that $l_q \leq l < l_{q+1}$, with $0 = l_0 < l_1 < ... < l_{p-1} < l_p = Z$. But the computation of layer l involves the samples of slices l and $l+1$, plus the samples of slices $l-1$ and $l+2$ for the computation of the centered gradient. From these remarks, we deduce that processor q needs the slices between $l_q - 1$ and $l_{q+1} + 1$, wherever these indices make sense.

We explain now how the surface is generated in parallel, so as to keep it non-redundant, and with each vertex associated with a unique global number ranging between 0 and $\mathcal{V} - 1$. The algorithm proceeds into three steps performed by each processor on its sub-domain:

1. Determination of the vertex offset.
2. Computation of the local surface.
3. Communication and update of shared vertex indices.

We give now some more details about each of these three steps:

Determination of the vertex offset: Each processor needs to number each vertex generated with a unique global index. In the previous steps of the algorithm, (see above in this section and in Sec. 2.3), we have already computed how many vertices will be generated on each horizontal layer. If these numbers are redistributed together with the image slices during the load-balancing step, all what we need is to perform a parallel prefix sum of these quantities to know the number of vertices (called the *vertex offset*) that will be generated by the predecessor of the current processor. This processor will thus generate indexes starting from this offset.

Computation of the local surface: This step is simply the execution of the sequential Marching-Cubes algorithm on the layers present on each processor. Since we want to keep the surface non-redundant, some of the vertices of the local surface are computed by neighboring processors. On processor q, the vertices belonging to slice l_q are computed by processor $q - 1$. Therefore, the triangles inside layer l_q, make reference to temporary vertex indices, that will be updated by the following step.

Communication and update of shared vertex indices: Each processor $q \neq p - 1$, sends to its successor the exact reference of vertices belonging to slice l_{q+1}. Each processor $q \neq 0$ receives thus the vertex indices of slice l_q. We are now ready to replace in the list of triangles of layer l_q the temporary vertex indices by their real reference.

Thanks to this communication step, the surface we produce is non-redundant and is exactly the same as the one produced by the sequential version. In Ref. 5, the author prefers to make redundant computations than communicating the shared vertices. Since we do not communicate the vertices themselves but only a reference to them, the cost of the message is very low (only four bytes per vertex), whereas its computation would require about 20 floating-point operations. We believe that the strategy of communicating rather than recomputing is more efficient. Moreover, for a small recoding effort, this communication could be easily overlapped with computations, and thus come for free.

4. EXPERIMENTS AND RESULTS

In this section, we present graphical outputs of the algorithm. Then we move to performance evaluation, comparing the sequential timings with those of the parallel version, with static and dynamic allocations.

Figure 5 was computed from a $256 \times 256 \times 113$ volumic image. The surface is composed of 583952 triangles and 293649 vertices. Note that the ratio $\mathcal{T}/\mathcal{V}$ is much smaller than the upper bound $\gamma = 8/3$ of Sec. 2.3, which is approached only for very specific artificial images.

In our first numerical experiment, we want to illustrate the usefulness of our load-balancing strategy. We use an artificial image where the number of vertices along the z axis respects a gaussian repartition. We use a Paragon with 8 processors, and we plot the load of each processor using a static allocation (equi-repartition of the data) and our dynamic redistribution scheme (equi-repartition of the workload). We clearly see in Fig. 6 that the unbalanced execution time is much higher than the balanced one, despite the time spent in the redistribution. This figure also shows the validity of our model used to predict the execution time as a function of the number of generated vertices.

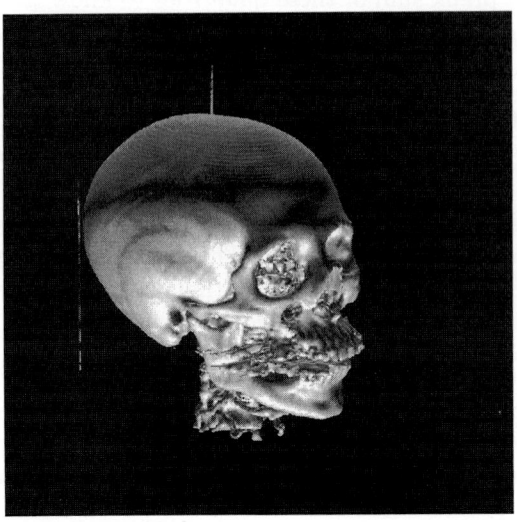

Fig. 5.   Rendering of a CT skull.

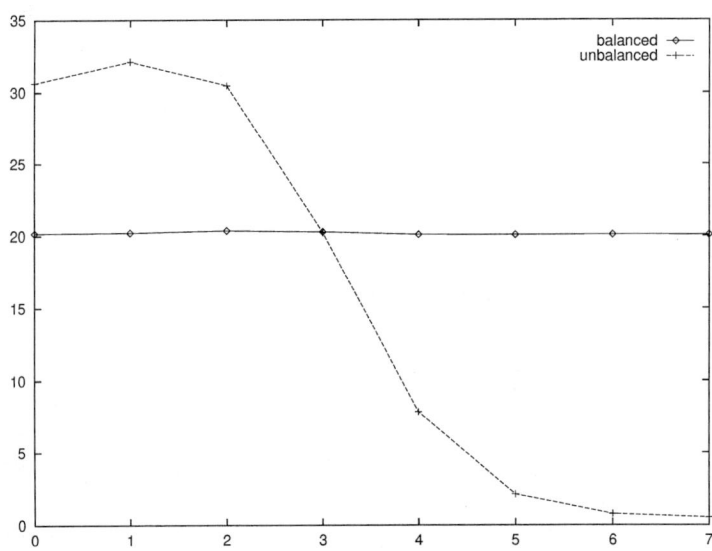

Fig. 6.   Workload of each processor. Static allocation versus dynamic redistribution.

Finally, we plot in Fig. 7, the speedup of the parallel algorithm as a function of the number of processors, both for the static and dynamic allocation. Our test image is a computed tomographic image of a skull. Of course, the improvement of the dynamic version is not as spectacular for this medical image as for the synthetic image of Fig. 6, but we observe nevertheless a significant improvement of the results.

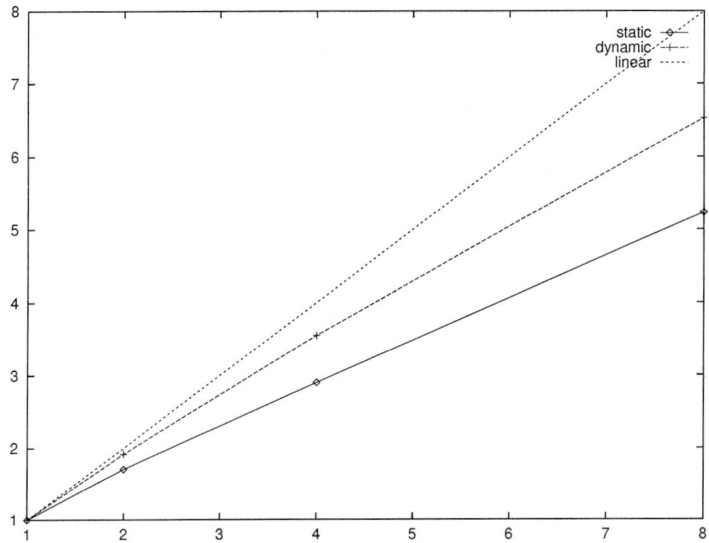

Fig. 7.   Speedup of the algorithm. Static allocation versus dynamic redistribution.

5. DISCUSSION

5.1. Improving the Load-Balance Precision

The previous experiments show the efficiency of our implementation, that allows to measure interesting speedups at least for small configuration machines. Nevertheless, the simple solution that consists in partitioning the layers of the 3D image on a linear network of processors must be reconsidered in the case of a massively parallel machine, having a number of processors comparable or even greater to the number of input slices. Indeed, each processor would be initially allocated a small number of input layers (or even no layer at all if there are more processors than the greatest dimension of the image). The scalability of our solution wouldn't be ensured. We are thinking of slight modifications to our algorithm for the case of large configuration machines.

A first solution would be to use 2D or 3D allocations of the data, on 2D or 3D meshes of processors. But it is well known that load-balancing on these kinds of interconnection networks is very hard to perform when locality constraints apply to the data.

We think rather about generalizing our 1D allocation scheme in the following way: The elastic load-balancing algorithm gives the integer frontier indices denoted l_q and l_{q+1} for processor q in the analysis of Sec. 3.2. Remember that processor q is thus responsible for the layers of indices l such that $l_q \leq l < l_{q+1}$. These integers are truncated values of the theoretical floating-point indices λ_q and λ_{q+1}.

Consider first the simple case where each processor is allocated at least one input layer (i.e. $l_q < l_{q+1}$, $\forall q \mid 0 \leq q < p$). We propose to allocate to processor q, the layers l such that $l_q \leq l \leq l_{q+1}$. In other words, layer l_{q+1} will be shared between processors q and $q + 1$. This small duplication of the data allows us to have a better precision for the quantity of work allocated to a processor: for instance, processor q computes only the fraction $\lambda_{q+1} - l_{q+1}$ of slice l_{q+1}, and the fraction $1 - (\lambda_q - l_q)$ of slice l_q.

Let us consider now the more general case where a processor would be allocated no data at all in the previous scheme, for instance because there are more processors than the number of input layers. This means that for a particular q, we have $l_q = l_{q+1}$. We propose to allocate the layer l_q to this processor, and to let it compute a fraction $\lambda_{q+1} - \lambda_q$ of this layer. In this scheme, a layer l is shared between all processors q such that $[\lambda_q, \lambda_{q+1}[\cap [l, l + 1[\neq \emptyset$.

5.2. Multiple Iso-Surface Extraction

We explained in Sec. 3.2 that our workload estimation directly depends on the number of vertices of the triangulation. In the framework of an interactive threshold selection, we would have to reestimate this number for each different value of the threshold. We briefly describe now a simple way to avoid the total rescanning of the data, and that allows to obtain immediately and for each threshold value, the number of vertices that will be present on each layer.

We replace the vertex number determination (see Sec. 2.3) by the following procedure: we maintain for each layer l, a 256 entries table $\mathcal{V}_l$ where $\mathcal{V}_l[t]$ holds the number of vertices that are going to be generated on the layer l for the threshold t. To construct these tables, only one scan of the data is needed. For a cell edge whose extremities have values v_1 and v_2 (assume without loss of generality that $v_1 \leq v_2$), we increment $\mathcal{V}_l[v]$ for all v between v_1 and $v_2 - 1$. A programming trick can be used to speed up this process: we increment $\mathcal{V}_l[v_1]$ and decrement $\mathcal{V}_l[v_2]$. Once the whole layer is processed, we scan sequentially $\mathcal{V}_l$ and replace $\mathcal{V}_l[k]$ by $\mathcal{V}_l[k-1] + \mathcal{V}_l[k]$, for $k = 1 \ldots 255$.

At the end of this preprocessing step, $\mathcal{V}_l[t]$ contains the number of vertices computed on layer l, for the triangulation corresponding to the threshold t. Therefore, the memory occupation, the workload estimation and the vertex index can be derived immediately for any chosen threshold.

6. CONCLUSION

We have presented in this paper a new parallel implementation of the Marching-Cubes algorithm on a distributed memory machine. We have shown how to compute a non-redundant surface with load balanced computations, which had not been done previously. One of the tasks that is added to the sequential algorithm consists in determining *a priori* the number of vertices that will be generated in the surface. We show that this small computation serves in three different steps of the algorithm: the determination of the size of the tables used to store the surface, the computation of the vertex offset used to give a unique index to each vertex, and the estimation of the workload that is a linear function of the number of vertices.

The two-level data structure we use is perfectly adapted to be input in a parallel rendering algorithm. In Ref. 1, Charles, Lefevre and Miguet present a load-balanced parallelization of the Z-Buffer algorithm using this data structure. The non-redundancy of the representation allows to have a minimal overhead for the geometric transformations of the vertices. The compact structure of the triangles allows to re-shuffle them efficiently in the machine for load-balancing purposes.

Finally, we want to mention that our code is written on the top of PPCM (for Portable Parallel Communication Module). This software environment developed at LIP includes a machine independent communication library integrating the elastic load-balancing redistribution. We have thus ported easily our application to several distributed memory machines as well as on networks of UNIX workstations.

REFERENCES

1. H.-P. Charles, L. Lefevre and S. Miguet, "An optimized and load-balanced portable parallel ZBuffer", in *SPIE Symp. Electronic Imaging: Science and Technology*, 1995.
2. F. Feschet, S. Miguet and L. Perroton, *CAPA: Parallélisme et Applications Irrégulières*, vol. 2, chapter ParList: une structure de donnée parallèle pour l'équilibrage des charges (in French), HERMES, 1995, pp. 177–201.
3. C. D. Hansen and P. Hanker, "Massively parallel isosurface extraction", in *Proc. IEEE Visualisation*, 1992, pp. 77–83.
4. W. E. Lorensen and H. E. Cline, "Marching cubes, a high resolution 3D surface construction algorithm", *Comput. Graphics* **21**, 4 (1987) 163–169.
5. P. Mackerras, "A fast parallel marching-cubes implementation on the fujitsu ap1000", Technical Report TR-CS-92-10, The Australian National University, August 1992.
6. S. Miguet and J.-M. Nicod, "A load-balanced parallel implementation of the marching-cubes algorithm", in *HPCS'95*, Montreal, 1995.
7. S. Miguet and Y. Robert, "Elastic load balancing for image processing algorithms", in *Parallel Computation*, ed. H. P. Zima, Lecture Notes in Computer Science, pp. 438–451, Salzburg, Austria, September 1991. 1st International ACPC Conference, Springer Verlag.
8. J. Wilhelms and A. Van Gelder, "Topological considerations in isosurface generation", *ACM Comput. Graphics* **24**, 5 (1990) 79–86.
9. M. Zheng and H. T. Nguyen, *An Efficient Parallel Implementation of the Marching-Cubes Algorithm*, Massively Parallel Processing Applications and Development, Institute of Systems Science, National University of Singapore, 1994, pp. 903–910.

Serge Miguet graduated in 1988 from the Ecole Nationale Superieure d'Informatique et de Mathématiques Appliquees de Grenoble (ENSIMAG). He obtained his PhD in 1990 from the Institut National Polytechnique de Grenoble (INPG) and his Diplome d'Habilitation à Diriger des Recherches in 1995 from the Universitè Claude Bernard de Lyon (UCBL). As an assistant professor at the Ecole Normale Superieure de Lyon (ENS-Lyon) since 1991, he has led a small group of researchers working on algorithmic/architectural parallel solutions for 3D medical imaging problems.

His main interests lie in studying methodologies for load-balancing data-parallel large scale computations. He became a professor at the Lyon-2 University in September 1996.

Jean-Marc Nicod received his Ph.D. degree in computer science from the Ecole Normale Supérieure de Lyon, France, in 1997. He has worked on parallel surface extraction in 3D medical images. He has been a postdoctoral researcher at the Ecole Normale Supérieure de Lyon and at the University Lumière Lyon 2. He is now an assistant professor at the IUT of Belfort-Montbeliard. His main scientific interests lie in the conception of parallel algorithms for 3D medical image processing.